Travel Guide To

Seville,
SPAIN

Escape to Spain: The Only Companion You Need!!

Wybikes Hinton

COPYRIGHT NOTICE

DISCLAIMER

Please note that the information contained within this document is for educational purposes only. The information contained herein has been obtained from sources believed to be reliable at the time of publication. The opinions expressed herein are subject to change without notice.

Readers acknowledge that the Author / Publisher is not engaging in rendering legal, financial or professional advice. The Publisher / Author disclaims all warranties as to the accuracy, completeness, or adequacy of such information.

The Publisher assumes no liability for errors, omissions, or inadequacies in the information contained herein or from the interpretations thereof. The publisher / Author specifically disclaims any liability from the use or application of the information contained herein or from the interpretations thereof.

TABLE OF CONTENT

Contents

WELCOME TO SEVILLE!

Seville! Just speaking the name evokes so many beautiful memories. This city, with its gleaming sunlight, twisting alleyways, and vivid flamenco rhythms, will steal your heart, as it has mine. Whether you're here for the history, the food, or simply to lose yourself in the warm embrace of Andalusian charm, you're in for a treat. But, before you dig into this cultural melting pot, let me give you a little overview of what to expect when you arrive in this fascinating city.

A Brief History of Seville

Seville's history is like a layered cake, with each slice exposing a new aspect of its interesting past. From the Romans to the Moors and, finally, the Spanish Crown, each epoch has left its stamp on the city. The Romans created Seville as Hispalis, and if you've ever walked through its historic alleyways, you'll feel like you've stepped into a movie set where history and legend collide. The city's strategic location on the banks of the Guadalquivir River made it an important commerce center. In fact, it became a hub of exploration and commerce during Spain's Golden Age in the 16th century.

However, the Moorish influence is particularly striking. It can be found in the landmark Alcázar palace, exquisite tiles on historic houses, and the small winding lanes of the Santa Cruz area. The city's architecture is a fascinating mix of Mudejar, Gothic, Renaissance, and Baroque styles, but the Islamic-inspired Mudejar is what gives Seville its unique character.

When to Visit: Best Time of Year

They say timing is everything. When it comes to Seville, time can mean the difference between a relaxing stroll around sunlit plazas and anxiously seeking shade like a vampire caught off guard at morning.

The finest times to visit Seville are in the spring and October. From March to May, the city is alive with vivid flowers, fresh orange blossoms (the smell is overpowering), and the exciting pageantry of Semana Santa (Holy Week) and Feria de Abril (April Fair). During these months, temperatures remain around a pleasant 20-25°C (68-77°F), ideal for strolling through the Alcázar gardens or people-watching at a café in Plaza Nueva.

If you enjoy blistering heat, travel in July or August— just keep in mind that people will be primarily indoors in air-conditioned comfort, leaving you with the city (and its 40°C (104°F) temperatures) to yourself. Personally, I recommend avoiding this time period unless you enjoy heat waves; however, if you do visit during the summer, take advantage of Seville's rooftop pools and late-night tapas culture when the city comes alive after midnight.

Another pleasant season is autumn, which lasts from September to November. The searing heat has subsided, and you can attend some of Seville's most lovely neighborhood festivals. Winter isn't that bad either—imagine enjoying hot chocolate and churros in a warm café while avoiding the summer throng.

Getting To Seville: Flights, Trains, and Buses

So, how do you go to this Andalusian jewel? Fortunately, Seville is well-connected, making it quite easy to get there—whether by plane, rail, or beautiful bus.

If you're flying in, Seville Airport (Aeropuerto de Sevilla-San Pablo) is only a 20-minute drive from the city center. Most European cities have regular flights, and there are even some direct flights from North America, however many tourists choose to connect in Madrid or Barcelona. A taxi from the airport to your hotel should cost roughly 20 euros, or you can take a shuttle bus for a few euros if you want to preserve your travel money for tapas.

Trains are another excellent alternative. Renfe's high-speed AVE trains connect Seville to Madrid in approximately 2.5 hours, which means you could be in Madrid for breakfast and back in Seville by late lunch! The Santa Justa train station is conveniently positioned near the city center. And if you're a romantic like me who enjoys the concept of unhurried travel, bus services throughout Spain are dependable, with pleasant options like as Alsaor Socibus providing routes from adjacent cities.

First Impression: What to Expect

Now, let's talk about the initial few moments after your arrival. Seville greets you as if you're a long-lost friend. The warmth, both symbolic and actual, strikes you immediately. The streets are busy, but not in a crazy, overwhelming way. Instead, everything flows rhythmically, as if the city is dancing to an unheard flamenco beat. And don't be surprised if you hear a faint strum from a guitar somewhere in the distant. It's Seville's way of informing you that you've arrived in a city where music and passion flow through every nook.

Your senses will be on high alert: the vivid hues of Seville's ceramic tiles, the perfume of orange trees bordering the streets, the cool breeze from the Guadalquivir River—it's all a little intoxicating. If you're like me, you'll be tempted to do one of two things: walk directly to the local café for a coffee and people-watching session, or dash to the Plaza de España for the first Instagram-worthy image. Go ahead; Seville will not mind. It's the type of city that you may explore at your own pace.

Practical Tips for First-time Visitors

Okay, let's get practical. Seville is a dream, but every dream requires a little preparation to avoid nightmares. Here are several lessons I learned the hard way that will save you time, money, and possibly a sunburn or two.

1. Stay hydrated!Even in the spring, the Andalusian sun is harsh. Always carry a bottle of water with you, especially if you're visiting outdoor attractions. Seville has numerous fountains where you may refill—look for the antique ones near public areas.

2. Siesta is real, and tourists can enjoy afternoon naps. Many shops and companies close between 2:00 and 5:00 p.m. for a well-deserved break. Use this time wisely: either embrace the siesta lifestyle and take a nap, or find a covered café to rest your

feet and recharge with some delicious tinto de verano (a chilled wine-based drink) while waiting for the city to awaken again.

3. Dress comfortably. Cobblestone streets and small alleys are charming, but they are not forgiving if you wear heels. Pack suitable walking shoes, as Seville is best experienced on foot.

4. Tapas timing: Remember that dinner in Spain is late—very late. Most locals won't eat dinner until 9:00 p.m. or later. If you're starving by 7:00 PM, opt for tapas instead. They're little plates designed for nibbling, but they can easily become a complete meal if you order enough of them!

5. Be patient with the flow of life. Things move slowly in Seville, which adds to the city's beauty. Don't rush—take your time, savor the moment, and allow Seville to reveal itself to you piece by piece.

Seville has a fascinating way of combining the past and present, making you feel as if you're part of a timeless story. As you enter this sun-kissed city, prepare to leave a piece of your heart behind, for Seville always leaves an impression on you, no matter how brief your visit.

Chapter 1

ACCOMMODATION

When planning a trip to Seville, the first significant question that comes to mind (after "how much tapas can I eat?") is where to stay. Seville, with its mix of old heritage and modern beauty, provides plenty of lodging options for all types of visitors. Whether you enjoy being pampered at a magnificent resort, are a budget-conscious explorer, or simply want to stay somewhere distinctive and unforgettable, Seville has something for you. I've stayed in a variety of hotels here, and I can tell you that the correct lodging can make or break your trip in this city. So let's have a look at Seville's lodgings, where you'll quickly realize that there's much more to housing than just a bed and breakfast.

Overview of Accommodation Options

Seville has a wide range of housing options to suit different interests and budgets. There's something for everyone, from opulent resorts that treat you like royalty to quirky boutique guesthouses where the personal touches make all the difference. Seville has something for everyone, whether you're looking for luxury or a budget-friendly vacation. And I mean that literally—some of the places here will make you feel as if you've walked into someone's carefully decorated living room.

Seville's accommodations are dispersed throughout several districts, each with its own distinct flavor. Would you like to stay in the historic Santa Cruz neighborhood? Or how about a stylish apartment overlooking the fashionable Triana neighborhood? Deciding where to stay is about more than just comfort; it's also about immersing yourself in the city's unique moods.

Luxury Resorts

If you enjoy the finer things in life, Seville's luxury resorts will feel like your own personal palace. Believe me when I say that these places know how to treat. The luxury hotels in Seville are opulent, with several housed in centuries-old palaces and featuring breathtaking courtyards, rooftop pools, and Michelin-starred dining. It's the kind of stay that will make you wonder whether you could live there forever (spoiler: probably not, but a traveler can dream).

1. Hotel Alfonso XIII

- Address: Calle San Fernando 2, 41004 Seville.

- If Seville had royalty, they'd most likely reside in the 5-star Hotel Alfonso XIII, one of Spain's most famous establishments, located just steps from Seville Cathedral and the Alcázar. The hotel's spectacular Moorish-style architecture will have you gawking as soon as you walk in. With intricate gardens, magnificent tile work, and chambers that appear to have been created for a sultan, here is luxury at its finest. And have I mentioned the rooftop pool? Perfect for enjoying cocktails and admiring the skyline.

2. Eme Cathedral Hotel

- Address: Calle Alemanes 27, 41004 Seville.

- Eme Catedral Hotel, a sleek, contemporary 5-star resort with unsurpassed views of Seville's famed Giralda Tower, is ideal for visitors seeking a mix of elegance and modernity. I stayed here once and, believe me, nothing beats breakfast with that backdrop. The rooftop pool and terrace are a must-see, especially in the evening when the lights illuminate the cathedral. The hotel's mix of modern and historical style will make you feel like you're living in two different eras at once (in the greatest manner imaginable).

3. Gran Meliá Colón

Location: Calle Canalejas, 1, 41001 Seville.

- If you enjoy art, culture, and elegance, Gran Meliá Colón will meet all of your needs. This hotel exudes elegance, from its avant-garde design to the famous Spanish paintings on its walls. It is located in the El Arenal district, so you are right in the thick of the action, with easy access to popular attractions. Furthermore, they provide a pillow menu—yes, a pillow menu—because why settle for one style of pillow when you may have a dozen options?

Budget-Friendly Hotels

For those of us who like to spend our euros on jamón ibérico and flamenco shows rather than on lodging, Seville has lots of affordable hotels that don't sacrifice comfort or charm. Staying on a budget does not imply missing out on the essence of Seville. There are numerous low-cost lodging options that provide clean, comfortable accommodations with a touch of local character.

1. Hotel Bécquer

- Address: Calle Reyes Católicos 4, 41001 Seville.

- I enjoy this place because it is inexpensive but does not feel like a sacrifice. Hotel Bécquer has nice accommodations and is centrally located, making it easy to explore Seville on foot. You'll be near the Guadalquivir River and just a short walk from the cathedral. The rooftop terrace with views of the Giralda is an unexpected perk for a hotel at this price point. It's clean, convenient, and provides everything you need without breaking the bank.

2. Hostal Giralda Sta. Cruz

Location: Calle de la Gloria, 7, 41004 Seville.

- Hostal Giralda, located in the heart of the Santa Cruz area, is a charming budget alternative that is just a stone's throw away from the Giralda Tower and Alcázar. The rooms are modest but comfortable, and the location? Totally unbeatable. It's ideal for anyone wishing to be in the thick of historical events without spending a fortune. Furthermore, the area's winding streets will make you feel like you're in a genuine Spanish soap opera.

3. Pension Catedral

- Address: Calle de los Tintes 22, 41003 Seville.

- This little pension is suitable for guests who only require the basics: a clean bed, a private bathroom, and closeness to the sites. It's a little off the main tourist trail, so you'll get a more local vibe. I stayed here on my first trip to Seville, and while it was not luxury, it was ideal for what I needed: a quiet, affordable place to bed after a full day of sightseeing.

Boutique Guesthouses

If you're looking for something with a little more personality, Seville has plenty of boutique guesthouses that provide a more intimate, personalized experience. These are frequently run by locals, and staying in one can feel like you've been invited into someone's (quite fashionable) house. These establishments typically have high-end décor with meticulous attention to detail, as well as warm and pleasant service.

1. Corral del Rey

- Address: Calle Corral del Rey 12, 41004 Seville.

Corral del Rey embodies the essence of boutique appeal. This old 17th-century palace, tucked away on a quiet street in the Alfalfa area, has been wonderfully refurbished and offers the ideal combination of antique grandeur and modern comfort. The rooftop terrace features a tiny plunge pool, and each room is beautifully adorned with beautiful artwork. It's private, luxurious, and feels like a hidden treasure.

2. Palacio Pinello

- Address: Calle Segovias 1, 41004 Sevilla.

Palacio Pinello, a lovely boutique hotel set in a former noble mansion, is located in the heart of the city, just a few steps away from the cathedral. The apartments are all tastefully designed, with original touches such as vaulted ceilings and wooden beams. Furthermore, the personnel here is fantastic—they go out of their way to make your stay memorable, from personalized restaurant recommendations to arranging private sightseeing tours.

3. La casa del maestro

- Location: Calle Niño Ricardo 5, 41003 Seville.

- La Casa del Maestro, a modest boutique hotel in the La Encarnación neighborhood, was formerly the home of a well-known flamenco guitarist, and it is still filled with his energy. The rooms are a blend of old and contemporary styles, with a strong sense of history in every corner. I enjoyed the cozy ambiance, and the rooftop patio is an excellent place to relax after a day of touring. It's the kind of location that makes you feel like you've uncovered a little piece of true Sevilla.

Unique Stays

Want to stay somewhere genuinely unforgettable? Seville is a city that understands how to be unique. There are numerous venues that provide an out-of-the-ordinary stay, ranging from old convents converted into hotels to avant-garde architectural masterpieces. These one-of-a-kind accommodations are ideal for guests who want their stay to be an adventure in and of itself.

1. El Rey Moro Hotel Boutique.

- Address: Calle Reinoso 8, 41004 Sevilla.

- Imagine staying in a classic Andalusian mansion with a stunning central courtyard adorned with orange trees and trickling fountains. El Rey Moro is a lovely boutique hotel in the Santa Cruz area that is just as magical as the name implies. The building goes back to the 16th century, and each chamber is uniquely adorned with whimsical details. What is the best part?

You can borrow one of their bikes for free and explore Seville at your leisure.

2. Hotel Ateneo

- Address: Calle Angostillo 10, 41003 Sevilla.

- Staying at the Hotel Ateneo is like walking into a work of art. This property is extravagant in the best manner conceivable, with sumptuous decor, antique furniture, and a large library straight out of a historical drama. Located in the center of Seville's old town, it's the ideal place to stay if you want to experience something as unique as the city itself. Every time I walked through the foyer, I felt like I was an extra in a beautiful historical film.

3. Patio de la Alameda

- Location: Plaza Alameda de Hércules 56, 41002 Seville.

- If you want to stay in one of Seville's most lively neighborhoods, go no farther than Patio de la Alameda. This hotel, located immediately on the busy Alameda de Hércules, is set in a historic 19th-century edifice that was previously a nobleman's home. The accommodations surround a gorgeous inner courtyard, and the neighborhood is brimming with clubs, restaurants, and nightlife. It's an excellent location for those who wish to absorb up the local culture.

Top Recommended Hotels and Resorts

With so many alternatives, it can be difficult to determine which destinations are worth your valuable vacation time. Based on my experiences (and a few talks with other visitors), these are the top recommended locations to stay, depending on your needs:

- For luxury, Hotel Alfonso XIII is unquestionably the best choice. The sheer magnificence of the place will make you feel like royalty.

- For budget tourists, Hotel Bécquer provides an excellent blend of price, comfort, and location.

- For a one-of-a-kind experience, the El Rey Moro Hotel Boutique will take you back in time with its stunning Andalusian courtyard and lovely atmosphere.

Choosing the Right Accommodation for You

Choosing the appropriate hotel in Seville comes down to the type of experience you seek. Are you come to indulge in luxury, or do you prefer something more warm and intimate? Do you want to be in the middle of the action or somewhere quieter? Take some time to consider what matters to you—whether it's a rooftop pool, historical charm, or closeness to tapas bars—and you'll find the ideal location.

Booking Tips & Tricks

Before you rush to make your reservation, allow me to provide some advice. First and foremost, whether you're traveling during Semana Santa or the Feria de Abril, make sure to book in advance. The city becomes overcrowded, and costs increase. Second, use booking services like as Booking.com or Airbnb to compare prices, but always check the hotel's own website as well—they may offer exclusive bargains. Finally, if you're on a tight budget, consider reserving mid-week stays instead of weekends, which are typically more expensive.

There you have it! Seville's hotel options are as varied and intriguing as the city itself. Whether you're looking for a stately retreat or a quirky guesthouse, Seville has the ideal location to unwind after a day of touring its picturesque streets. And believe me, after a day of roaming the cobblestones of Santa Cruz or climbing the Giralda Tower, you'll appreciate having a cozy place to return to—whether it has a rooftop pool or just a comfortable bed.

Chapter 2

NAVIGATING SEVILLE

Getting about Seville is similar to learning to dance flamenco. It can be daunting at first, but once you get your rhythm, you'll be gliding through the city like you've been doing it your entire life. Whether you prefer the modern comfort of public transit or prefer to walk through the streets, Seville provides a number of options for getting from point A to point B. But don't be surprised if you get lost in the city's beauty—that's sort of the goal.

Allow me to share some of my experiences with Seville's transportation environment, from using the trams to cycling through the tight streets. Along the way, I'll share some tips and tactics that I've learned (often the hard way), and perhaps, by the conclusion of this chapter, you'll be ready to traverse Seville like a native. If all else fails, remember to follow the fragrance of tapas.

Public Transportation: Buses, Trams, and Metro

First and foremost, if you want to use public transportation in Seville, you will be delighted to discover that it is extremely well-organized and reasonably priced. The city features a well-organized network of buses, trams, and a metro system that makes getting around simple—especially when your feet are aching from hours of wandering.

Buses

Seville's bus system is enormous, spanning much of the city, including several areas that are difficult to reach by foot. The buses are contemporary, air-conditioned, and most importantly, frequent. You won't have to wait long at the bus stop, which is ideal because, while Seville's weather is normally pleasant, standing in the sun in August may feel like you're roasting in an oven. Believe me, I've been there.

If you plan on staying for more than a few days, I recommend buying a Tussam card (the local bus pass). It's a rechargeable card that makes getting on and off buses simple. It costs less per ride than cash and can also be used on trams.

Some important bus routes to remember:

- Bus 21: This route takes you from the historic center to the Nervión shopping zone. If you want to mix sightseeing and shopping, this is the ride for you.

- Bus C1/C2: These circular routes wrap around the city, providing an excellent overview of Seville's layout. It's like a low-cost city tour!

Bus stops are clearly marked, and there is generally a digital display indicating how long before the next bus arrives. However, in Spain, things occasionally run on "Spanish time," so give or take a few minutes.

Trams

Oh, the tram! When I'm too lazy to walk yet don't want to take the bus, this is probably my favorite way to travel around the city. Seville's tram system is modest (just one line), but it's really useful, especially if you're staying in the city center.

The MetroCentro tram connects some of Seville's major attractions. It stretches from Plaza Nueva, near the cathedral, to San Bernardo, going via the Puerta de Jerez. The tram's appeal is that it is speedy, dependable, and, as an added bonus, excellent for people watching. If you're staying anywhere near the old district, you'll probably be able to catch the tram in minutes.

I once took the tram all the way to the end of the line without realizing it (I was so focused in watching a bunch of youngsters play spontaneous flamenco in the street). Fortunately, the trams run often, so I was back on my way quickly.

Metro

Seville's metro system is relatively new and significantly smaller than other large cities, having only one line (so far). But don't be fooled—it's a very useful way to get around, especially if you're going to places farther away from the city center, such as Sevilla Esteor Mairena del Aljarafe.

The metro is clean, fast, and simple to use. The stations are contemporary, with sufficient of signage in Spanish and English. And here's a little secret: it's the ideal hideaway when the summer heat becomes oppressive. Pop below, enjoy the air conditioning, and emerge on the opposite side of the city, rested and eager to explore.

The metro has 22 stations, and tickets can be purchased from machines inside the stations. A single ride costs roughly 1.40 euros, but you may also obtain day passes if you plan to go frequently.

Walk Through the Historic Center

Here's the thing about Seville: it's designed for walking. Sure, you could take the subway or a tram, but nothing beats getting lost (deliberately or not) in the twisting streets of Barrio Santa Cruz or Triana. Walking is typically the best—and most enjoyable— way to navigate around the city's historic center, which is extremely tight.

Every nook in Seville is full with surprises. You might turn a corner and come into a small plaza filled with orange trees and folks chatting on seats. Or you can come face to face with an impromptu flamenco performance in the center of a cobblestone square. Seville rewards the curious walker, so take your time and stroll aimlessly for a little.

However, Seville's narrow, twisting streets can be disconcerting, particularly in districts like Santa Cruz, where passageways appear to twist and turn on themselves. I've lost track of how many times I've unintentionally walked in circles, just to return to where I began. But, truthfully, getting lost is half of the appeal. And when you finally emerge from a tangle of alleyways and find the Giralda Tower towering above you, you'll feel as if you've discovered it anew.

One piece of advice: wear comfortable shoes. The streets are lovely, however many are lined with cobblestones that can be harsh on feet (and heels). I discovered this the hard way, after wearing new sandals on my first day. A big mistake. By the end of the day, I was limping back to my hotel like a battered flamenco dancer.

Cycling in Seville: A Bicycle-Friendly City

Now, I will admit that I am not much of a cyclist. In fact, the last time I rode a bike before moving to Seville, I slammed into a mailbox. However, in Seville, cycling is essentially a way of life. The city has had a bicycle revolution in recent years, with over 170 kilometers of dedicated bike lanes. Even I, the clumsiest cyclist alive, felt safe riding down the spacious, tree-lined avenues.

If you're feeling daring, Sevici, Seville's bike-sharing system, is a great way to get around. You'll find these silver-and-blue bikes placed at docking stations all across town. Simply sign up at one of the kiosks, take a bike, and you're off! Sevici is ideal for short rides, especially since you may leave the bike at any station when you're finished.

Some excellent cycling routes include:

- Along the Guadalquivir River: There's a great bike trail that follows the river, with views of Triana and the Torre del Oro.

- Parque de María Luisa: Ideal for a leisurely cycling, with broad paths and ample shade. Just make sure to watch out for pedestrians.

If you want a more guided experience, various firms in Seville provide bike excursions. These are an excellent way to view the city while also getting some exercise—plus, you'll have a guide to ensure you don't unintentionally cycle into a busy street (which I may or may not have done on my first attempt).

Taxi and Ridesharing Options

When your feet can't take another step or you're rushing late for a flamenco show, taxis and rideshares are a quick and easy way to get around Seville. The city's cabs are plentiful, dependable, and reasonably priced in comparison to other European cities. They are easily identified by their white tint and yellow stripe.

To hail a taxi, you can either wave one down on the street or go to a taxi stand at a major location, such as Plaza de España or Santa Justa Train Station. Taxis use a meter system, and the charges are reasonable—though they do rise significantly at night or on public holidays. One night, after a full day of sightseeing, I got a taxi from Plaza Nuevaback to my hotel for approximately 7 euros, which seemed like a good deal given the ease.

Uber and Cabify are both available in Seville for those of us who are constantly connected to our smartphones. I frequently used Cabify since I found the app easy to use and the cars slightly more pleasant than normal taxis. The best thing is that you can see the price before confirming the ride, so there are no surprises at the end of the voyage.

Whether you take a taxi or a rideshare, it's comforting to know that if your legs give out or you accidently wander too far in the wrong direction (guilty), you'll have a comfy transport back to your hotel at your disposal.

Essential Apps for Getting Around

In the age of smartphones, there is an app for everything, including navigating Seville. Here are a few crucial apps that I found useful during my stay in the city. They'll save you time, frustration, and possibly even some bad turns:

TUSSAM App.

This is the official app for Seville's bus and tram systems, and it's really useful. It offers real-time bus arrival information, route maps, and neighboring stations. It even shows you how crowded the buses are, which is very useful at peak hours when you don't want to be squeezed in like sardines.

Sevici App

If you plan on cycling, the Sevici app is a must-have. It allows you to find the nearest docking stations and view the availability of bikes and parking spaces in real time. It also logs your rides, allowing you to brag to your pals about how much exercise you receive while sightseeing.

Cabify

Cabify is my go-to rideshare app. It operates similarly to Uber, although I thought the cars and service to be significantly superior. You can schedule rides ahead of time, view prices before booking, and even select your preferred car type.

Google Maps

I know—this one is a little apparent. But Google Maps in Seville is a game changer, especially when you're completely lost in a maze of narrow alleyways. The software gives walking, bicycle, and public transportation instructions, as well as the option to download offline maps if your data plan runs out.

So there you have it—a detailed guide on exploring Seville like a seasoned traveler. Whether you're taking a tram, cycling through the park, or wandering through the old district, the city has plenty of options to get around and discover its many attractions. Just remember to take your time, enjoy the journey, and don't be afraid to get a bit lost—after all, some of Seville's best moments occur while you're roaming aimlessly.

Chapter 3

SEVILLE'S ICONIC LANDMARKS (PART 1)

Seville is a city that understands how to showcase its splendor. The city's rich history is evident in every corner, from the towering Alcázar to the breathtaking Plaza de España. Whether you're strolling through a palace formerly occupied by Moorish kings or ascending a tower that has stood since the 12th century, you'll feel as if you've traveled back in time, only to be brought back to reality by the vivid life that surrounds these old landmarks.

Let's go on a tour of some of Seville's most recognizable landmarks. These are the sites you've probably seen on postcards and Instagram feeds, but nothing beats experiencing them firsthand. I've had the pleasure of visiting these locations several times, and each visit reveals something new. So lace up your comfortable shoes, take your camera (and a bottle of water), and let's go exploring.

Alcázar: A Moorish Marvel

Stepping into the Alcázaris is like going into a fantasy, one penned by both Moorish and Christian hands over ages. This palace, which was initially erected in the 10th century as a Moorish fort, is an architectural marvel that seamlessly combines Islamic art with Gothic and Renaissance features. It is also still used by the Spanish royal family, making it Europe's oldest royal residence in operation. How's that for some royal flair?

My first visit to the Alcázar made me feel as if I had been transported to another dimension. As I walked through the Patio de las Doncellas, with its finely carved arches and reflecting lakes, I almost expected to run into a medieval queen (or a Game of Thrones character—yes, they filmed some scenes here!). The Alcázar is a location where you can easily lose track of time as you explore its many rooms, courtyards, and gardens.

In terms of gardens, don't miss the Jardines del Alcázar, a magnificent tangle of fountains, palm trees, and hidden alcoves. These gardens are ideal for sitting, relaxing, and enjoying the soft air while contemplating what life was like for Moorish rulers who walked these same walks.

One tip: buy your tickets online in advance, especially during peak tourist season. The line might be as lengthy as a Spanish siesta. You don't want to spend half your day waiting in the sun while others are inside enjoying the scenery.

Seville Cathedral: Home of La Giralda

The massive Seville Cathedral, located close to the Alcázar, commands your attention from the moment you see it. This UNESCO World Heritage monument, the world's largest Gothic cathedral, inspires awe. When I initially stood in front of it, I couldn't help but tilt my head back and gape—this place is huge. The sheer enormity of the cathedral is amazing, but what really stands out is the meticulous craftsmanship that went into every element of the structure.

Inside, the cathedral is as breathtaking. The towering ceilings appear to reach indefinitely into the heavens, and the light that filters through the stained-glass windows creates vivid patterns on the stone floors. Visit Christopher Columbus' tomb, where the explorer's remains are claimed to rest. In any case, the monument is impressive, supported by four heraldic figures representing Spain's kingdoms.

The cathedral's bell tower, La Giralda, is one of Seville's most recognizable icons. Originally constructed as a minaret in the 12th century, it was later turned into a bell tower following the Reconquista. Climbing to the top is necessary, yet there are no stairs. Instead, you'll climb a series of ramps created so that the muezzin (the person who summons the devout to prayer) can ride a horse to the summit. When you get to the top, the sights are worth every step—or should I say ramp. The image of Seville's roofs extending out before you, with the Guadalquivir River twisting through the city, is stunning. Just prepare for a gust of wind at the top—I nearly lost my hat once!

Archivo de Indias

The Archivo de Indias, located between the Alcázar and the cathedral, is often overshadowed by its more famous neighbors but is equally fascinating. This inconspicuous structure houses one of the most significant collections of records pertaining to the Spanish Empire's exploration and colonization of the Americas. In fact, if you've ever wondered where all of the historical documents describing Columbus' voyages or the conquest of Mexico landed up, here is it.

The Archivo de Indias was formed in the 18th century to consolidate all papers distributed throughout Spain's colonies. In contrast to the grandeur of the Alcázar or cathedral, the structure itself is lovely in a more subtle manner. Inside, you'll find corridors lined with shelves holding nearly 43,000 volumes of documents—enough paper to fill more than nine kilometers of shelves!

While the archive is not a hands-on museum, it frequently holds fascinating exhibitions about Spain's colonial history. I went to an exhibit on the Spanish Armada once, and it was like being a fly on the wall during one of the most turbulent periods in Spanish history. If you are a history lover like me, this area is a goldmine.

Torre del Oro: The Golden Tower

Next, we travel to the banks of the Guadalquivir River, where the renowned Torre del Oro stands guard. The Almohads (who also built the Giralda's minaret) originally built this 13th-century watchtower to restrict river access to Seville. The tower's name, "Golden Tower," comes from the golden tint it reflected in the water due to the lime and straw mixture employed in its construction.

The Torre del Oro has had numerous lives. It began as a military watchtower, then became a prison, and is now home to a naval museum worth visiting if you're interested in Seville's nautical heritage. But, for me, the true charm of the Torre del Oro rests in the hike to the summit. From there, you may enjoy a stunning view of the river and its surroundings, including the historic Triananeighborhood across the water.

According to legend, the tower was once joined to a sister tower on the other side of the river by a massive chain intended to prevent ships from accessing the city. I think how dramatic it must have been to witness foes attempting (and failing) to storm the city by water.

A amusing situation occurred when I ascended the Torre del Oro with a friend who is afraid of heights. By the time we reached the top, he was clinging to the tower's side like a barnacle. Meanwhile, I was leaning over the side, hoping to get the ideal Instagram image of the river. Lesson learned: not everyone shares my fondness for high elevations!

La Maestranza, the Historic Bullring

Even if you don't like bullfighting, you can't discuss Seville without mentioning La Maestranza, the city's ancient bullring. This bullring, built in the 18th century, is one of Spain's most well-known and traditional. To be honest, bullfighting is a contentious issue, and I was unsure how I would feel about attending La Maestranza. However, the location's history and cultural value cannot be denied, and even if you do not watch a bullfight, the tour inside the arena is fascinating.

When I initially entered the ring, I was struck by the stark contrast between the bright, sandy arena and the whitewashed stands. It's a site steeped in tradition, with the crowd's cheers and gasps reverberating down the years. The bullring can seat over 12,000 people and is crowded to capacity during Seville's Feria de Abril.

The on-site museum provides information on the history of bullfighting in Seville, with exhibits featuring costumes, artwork, and even the heads of famous bulls (not for the faint-hearted!). Whether you enjoy the sport or not, the artistry and pageantry associated in bullfighting are distinctive to Spanish culture, and La Maestranza is at the center of it all.

Plaza de España, Seville's Crown Jewel

The Plaza de España is a must-see on any visit to Seville. This massive, semicircular plaza is the city's crown jewel, and with good cause. The Plaza de España, designed for the 1929 Ibero-American Exposition, combines Renaissance Revival and Moorish Revival styles. It features a central canal and bridges. If you think this sounds like a movie set, you're not far off—it has appeared in films such as Star Wars and Lawrence of Arabia.

I remember my first visit to Plaza de España. I arrived early in the morning, just as the sun was rising, putting a golden glow on the exquisite azulejos (painted ceramic tiles) that adorned the plaza walls. Each section of the plaza is dedicated to a different area of Spain, and you might spend hours admiring the intricate tilework that narrates the stories of each region.

Renting a rowboat is a popular tourist activity at the Plaza de España.

Paddle around the canal. Yes, it's cheesy, but I thoroughly enjoyed every minute of it. If rowing isn't your style, take a leisurely stroll around the plaza or sit by one of the numerous fountains to people-watch. The plaza is usually teeming with activity, with flamenco dancers performing for tips, couples having romantic boat rides, and families enjoying the sun.

These six landmarks are only the tip of the iceberg in terms of Seville's diverse cultural offerings. Each one offers a unique tale, incorporating centuries of history, art, and tradition into the city's fabric. Seville's icons, such as the Alcázar and Plaza de España, offer unforgettable experiences that last long after you depart. And the best part? There is yet more to discover in Part 2!

Chapter 4

SEVILLE'S ICONIC LANDMARKS (PART 2)

Seville is like that friend that constantly surprises you. Just when you think you've seen it all, they reveal another hidden treasure or architectural marvel that leaves you in awe. In this chapter, we'll explore some of Seville's lesser-known (but still beautiful) landmarks. These attractions may not necessarily be the first to appear in tourist brochures, but they are an important element of the city's soul. So, put on your walking shoes and accompany me for another journey across Seville's breathtaking ancient and modern wonders.

Metropol Parasol: Mushrooms of Seville

Let's begin with something absolutely modern and, honestly, a little strange—but in the greatest conceivable manner. Metropol Parasol, commonly known as "Las Setas" (The Mushrooms), is a huge wooden canopy that spans Plaza de la Encarnación. When I initially saw it, I assumed I'd stumbled upon a futuristic cityscape. It's weird to be standing in the heart of old Seville, looking up at this avant-garde gigantic mushroom canopy that appears to go on forever.

Metropol Parasol, designed by German architect Jürgen Mayer, is the world's largest wooden construction, both odd and beautiful. It's almost as if Seville chose to deviate from its conventional look for a minute and experiment with something bold, new, and surprising.

What's nice about Las Setas is that it's not only a unique landmark, but also functional. The archeological museum at the base allows visitors to see Roman and Moorish ruins found during the structure's construction. Above that, there's a bustling marketplace full of local sellers offering fresh produce, meats, and every Spanish cheese you can think of. The rooftop, however, is the real feature. You can take the elevator to the top and wander along a winding path for panoramic views of the entire city. Watching the sunset from up here is like seeing Seville shine from inside, with the Giralda tower boldly visible in the background. It's breathtaking—and possibly a little windy, so hold on to your hat!

Casa de Pilatos: A Noble Mansion

Casa de Pilatosis is one of those places that makes you question why it does not receive more recognition. Nestled in the center of Seville, this 16th-century palace is a spectacular mix of Mudejar and Renaissance architecture, and it is still privately held by the Medinaceli family. Fortunately for us, they have opened their doors so that the public can get a view of what aristocratic life in Seville would have been like.

Walking inside the gates of Casa de Pilatos is like going back in time. The palace is decorated with elegant azulejos (the beautiful, bright ceramic tiles that Seville is known for), intricate plasterwork, and lush gardens. The diversity of architectural forms pays homage to Seville's rich history of Moorish and Christian influences, and it serves as a reminder of how beautifully these two worlds clashed in one city.

The patio is my favorite feature of Casa de Pilatos. Consider this: a large marble fountain surrounded by palm palms, with sunlight flooding in through open archways and bouncing off the colorful tilework on the walls. It's so serene that you'll want to sit and take it all in. Don't forget to glance up! The ceilings in this area are pieces of art in their own right, with intricate carvings and murals that will leave you with a crick in your neck from staring up.

Casa de Pilatos is a must-see for anyone interested in history or magnificent architecture. If, like me, you've ever wondered what it's like to live in a palace, this is probably the closest you'll get without marrying into royalty.

Plaza de América and Parque María Luisa

Let's discuss about one of Seville's most lovely green spaces: Plaza de Américain and Parque de María Luisa. This park is the city's counterpart to Central Park—a sprawling, green sanctuary with shady walks, elegant fountains, and a diverse bird population that will make you feel like you've wandered into a nature documentary.

The Plaza de Américais is one of the park's centerpieces, but it is sometimes missed by visitors who head straight to the more famous Plaza de España. But let me tell you, Plaza de América has its own unique brand of charm. It is bordered by three superbly designed museum buildings: the Archaeological Museum, the Museum of Popular Arts, and the Royal Pavilion. Each of these structures is a masterpiece of Neo-Renaissance and Mudejar architecture, adding to the plaza's grandeur.

The first time I went, I spent hours walking about the park, watching residents paddle boats on the little lakes and couples walk hand in hand down the flower-lined walks. Then there are the pigeons—oh the pigeons. If you've ever wanted to mimic a scene from a Disney film in which birds rush around you in a frenzy, Plaza de América is the place. There's also a small booth where you can buy birdseed and feed the pigeons, which sounds nice until fifty of them sit on your shoulders at the same time. I felt like an extra in an Alfred Hitchcock movie!

The true beauty of Parque de María Luisa is its quiet. After navigating the city's hustle and bustle, it's the ideal spot to unwind, take a deep breath, and appreciate the natural beauty surrounding you.

Basilica of La Macarena

Seville is full with lovely churches, but the Basilica de la Macarena has a unique place in the hearts of many Sevillanos. This church, located in the Macarena area, houses one of the city's most famous figures: the Virgin of Hope of Macarena (also known as La Macarena). This statue of the Virgin Mary is notable for her lifelike tears and beautiful clothes, and she is a key figure in Seville's Semana Santa (Holy Week) processions.

Even if you are not religious, the church is worth a visit just to see the magnificent statue of La Macarena up close. The first time I saw her, I was struck by how passionate her expression is—her face is filled with pain, yet there is also something extremely serene about her. During Semana Santa, La Macarena is paraded through Seville's streets, drawing large crowds. It's an emotionally charged occasion, and the people's dedication is evident.

The church is a stunning example of Baroque architecture, with exquisite altarpieces and gilded embellishments. The main altar, where La Macarena sits, is a dazzling display of gold and gems. If you're lucky enough to visit during a quieter period, the basilica provides a serene setting in which to reflect or simply wonder at the creativity around you.

San Telmo Palace

Palacio de San Telmois is one of Seville's most magnificent buildings, but it often goes unnoticed by tourists. This 17th-century Baroque mansion, which served as a university for navigators during Spain's Golden Age of Exploration, is currently home to the Andalusian Autonomous Government. San Telmo is noteworthy for more than only its political purpose; the palace's history and design are what truly stand out.

The first thing I saw about San Telmo was its magnificent façade. It's decorated with intricate carvings and sculptures, with a towering central arch that can't be missed. The palace's striking red and white color scheme contributes to its majesty, setting it apart even in a city rich with stunning buildings.

San Telmo is also associated with myths and legends. There is a tale that the building was cursed after its architect, Leonardo de Figueroa, died unexpectedly while working on it. Whether or not you believe in curses, the palace exudes a sense of mystery.

Though the palace's interior is normally closed to the public, it does periodically open its doors for guided tours. If you're lucky enough to acquire a space, you'll be able to visit some of the exquisite chambers within, such as the Salón de los Retratos, which displays images of all prior Andalusian presidents.

The Hospital de Los Venerables

Finally, we visit one of Seville's hidden gems: the Hospital de los Venerables. Located in the heart of the Barrio Santa Cruz, this 17th-century edifice was originally a retirement house for elderly priests, but it is now an art center and a stunning example of Baroque architecture.

The Hospital de los Venerables may not appear impressive from the outside, but once inside, you are met by a magnificent courtyard surrounded by arched arcades. The tranquil environment here is a nice contrast to the busy streets outside, and the gardens are adorned with aromatic flowers and splashing fountains.

Inside the structure, you'll find an extraordinary collection of Spanish art, including works by the renowned Baroque painter Bartolomé Esteban Murillo, who was born in Seville. The chapel is another highlight, with its ornately painted ceilings and magnificent murals. I recall sitting in the chapel for a few seconds, enjoying the fine details of the artwork and feeling utterly relaxed. This is one of

Those locations that appear to take you to another time.

The Velázquez Center, housed within the hospital, is dedicated to the life and work of renowned painter Diego Velázquez, another well-known Sevillian. It's a small but intriguing museum ideal for art aficionados, providing a more intimate experience than some of the city's larger galleries.

As we conclude Part 2 of Seville's renowned landmarks, it becomes evident that this city is rich in history, art, and architectural wonders. Whether you're admiring Metropol Parasol's contemporary design or getting lost in the gardens of the Hospital de los Venerables, each of these landmarks provides insight into Seville's rich and diverse history. And the best part? There's always something new to uncover around each bend.

Chapter 5

THINGS TO DO IN SEVILLE (DAYTIME ACTIVITIES)

Seville is a city that invites you to explore from the moment the sun rises above the Guadalquivir River, casting golden light on the rooftops, until the final rays fade behind the Giralda. There's something beautiful about Seville during the day, when the streets are alive with activity, history whispers from every corner, and the perfume of orange blossoms seems to follow you everywhere. Whether you're a history buff, a foodie, or simply enjoy soaking up local culture, Seville has plenty of daily activities to keep you busy. So let's look at some of the best ways to spend your time in this Andalusian treasure.

River Cruises Around the Guadalquivir

One of my favorite ways to start the day in Seville is with a relaxing sail down the Guadalquivir River. There's something quite calming about gliding down the lake and watching the city unfold before you. The river has been a lifeblood for Seville since ancient times, and as you travel along, you'll see a mix of old structures and modern developments that illustrate the tale of the city's growth.

I recall my first river trip, sitting on the deck with a cool tinto de verano (that lovely mix of red wine and lemon soda), marveling at the contrast between the Moorish Torre del Oroon on one side and the sleek, modern Puente de la Barqueta on the other. The boat glided by the colorful houses of Triana, a district known for its pottery and flamenco, before heading to Isla de la Cartuja, the site of the 1992 World Expo.

Most river tours last approximately an hour, giving you ample time to take in the sights and gain a unique perspective on Seville without feeling confined to the boat. You'll travel by the Plaza de Toros, Seville's famous bullring, and have spectacular views of the San Telmo Palace and the Maestranza Theater. The commentary is frequently in many languages, but don't worry if you fall asleep for a moment while watching the river ripple in the sunlight—I've done it more times than I like to confess.

If you're feeling daring, kayak rentals are available along the river, which is a fantastic way to work off some of the tapas you've been indulging in. However, I prefer to leave the heavy work to the boat's captain while I relax and enjoy the journey.

Walking Tours in Seville's Historic Quarters

Seville is one of those cities where being lost is half the pleasure, especially when exploring the old areas. However, if you want to ensure that you don't miss any of the hidden jewels (or, to be honest, if your sense of direction is as bad as mine), a guided walking tour is the way to go.

Barrio Santa Cruz, or the historic Jewish district, is one of the nicest neighborhoods to explore on foot. This region is a maze of little alleyways, hidden courtyards, and stunning plazas, each more lovely than the last. I've gone lost in Santa Cruz so many times that I've lost count, but each wrong turn leads to something new—a delightful small café, a breathtaking view of the Alcázar, or a tiny square surrounded by orange trees. The guides are usually local specialists who know all the best sites and can tell you fascinating anecdotes about the area's history that you won't find in any guidebook.

Another place worth investigating is Triana, which is located across the river from the main city. Triana has a particular personality—gritty, energetic, and full of character. This neighborhood previously housed sailors, potters, and flamenco dancers, and its impact on Seville's culture cannot be understated. As you travel through the streets, you will notice historic ceramic workshops where artists have been creating colorful tiles for decades. And, if you're lucky, you might see a spontaneous flamenco performance in one of the nearby bars.

Walking tours are an excellent method to learn about Seville's history. One trip I took highlighted the city's Moorish past, with stops at sights such as the Giralda Tower and the Alcázar. It's astonishing how much more you enjoy these structures when you know the tales behind them—for example, how the Giralda was originally a mosque's minaret, or how the Alcázar's beautiful tilework demonstrates Mudejar artisans' craftsmanship.

Flamenco Dance Classes

Now let's talk about something that will get your heart racing: flamenco. You cannot visit Seville without experiencing the raw emotion and intensity of flamenco. However, watching a performance is one thing; learning to dance is another (and far sweatier) experience.

I'll admit that I'm not much of a dancer. In fact, the last time I tried to dance, I fell and almost knocked over a potted plant. But when in Seville, you must experience flamenco. There are many flamenco schools in the city that provide beginner sessions, and believe me, you don't need any prior expertise to participate. The instructors are very patient (luckily, in my situation), and they will walk you through the fundamentals of flamenco footwork, hand movements, and rhythms.

My first class was held in a modest studio in Triana, the hub of Seville's flamenco scene. The teacher, a feisty Sevillana named Carmen, clapped her hands to the beat and yelled instructions in fast Spanish while I struggled to catch up. The entire experience was amazing and hilarious, especially when I realized I had the coordination of a baby giraffe.

Despite not being prepared to perform on stage at La Carbonería, I learned fundamental flamenco steps and gained a new appreciation for the art form. And, of course, I was saturated in perspiration, which made the post-class tapas and wine taste even better.

Shopping at Triana and the Old Town

If you're like me, no trip is complete without some retail therapy. Shopping in Seville is more than simply buying souvenirs; it's also about discovering the city's artisanal traditions and distinctive local items.

For a genuinely unique shopping experience, visit Triana, a district noted for its pottery. Shops along Calle Alfarería provide hand-painted tiles, vases, dishes, and more. These objects are works of art in and of themselves, and many of the stores have been passed down through generations. I bought a few tiles as souvenirs during one of my trips, and they now stand proudly in my kitchen as a daily reminder of Seville's artistry.

If ceramics aren't your thing, don't worry: Seville's Old Town has plenty of other shopping options. Calle Sierpes and Calle Tetuán are the city's main shopping streets, with a mix of international brands and local businesses. I enjoy meandering down these pedestrianized lanes, stopping into shops to look at everything from fashion to jewelry to traditional mantillas (lace headscarves worn by women during religious processions).

For something a little more unique, visit the Mercado de la Feria, one of the city's oldest markets. This lively market is ideal for buying fresh fruit, local cheeses, and handcrafted items. I once spent an entire morning here, eating olives and cheeses and conversing with the pleasant stall owners, who were eager to share their recommendations for the best local specialties.

Visit Seville's Museums

Of course, no vacation to Seville is complete without visiting the city's numerous museums to learn about its rich cultural legacy. Whether you're interested in fine art, history, or archaeology, Seville's museums provide an intriguing look at the city's past and present.

The Museo de Bellas Artes is one of Seville's most well-known museums, set in a magnificent former convent. The building itself is worth a visit, with its huge courtyards and stunning architecture. Inside, you'll discover an outstanding collection of Spanish art, including pieces by Murillo, Zurbarán, and Velázquez. The museum's collection ranges from the medieval period to the twentieth century, but it is the Baroque pieces that truly stand out. On my first visit, I spent hours here, captivated by the dramatic lighting and emotion shown in the paintings.

For something more unique, visit the Centro Andaluz de Arte Contemporáneo on Isla de la Cartuja. This museum focuses on modern and contemporary art and is built in a former monastery that was later converted into a ceramics factory. The juxtaposition of the ancient and new creates an engaging environment, and the museum's displays frequently challenge traditional concepts of art. I once attended an exhibit of sculptures made completely of recycled materials that was both eccentric and thought-provoking.

If you enjoy history, visit the Museo Arqueológico in the Parque de María Luisa. This museum houses an amazing collection of antiquities from Seville's Roman and Moorish periods, including mosaics, pottery, and ancient sculptures. It's an intriguing look into civilizations that once called

Seville is home, and it's easy to lose track of time wandering around the galleries, imagining life in old Hispalis (the Roman name for Seville).

Seville comes alive during the day, with vibrant streets, ancient landmarks, and a dynamic environment. Whether you're riding down the

Guadalquivir, learning to flamenco, or getting lost in the old town's meandering lanes, there's always something fresh and intriguing to see. So take your time, soak it all in, and don't be afraid to get lost— that's when you'll discover Seville's true enchantment.

Chapter 6

WHAT TO DO IN SEVILLE (EVENING ACTIVITIES)

If Seville is lovely during the day, it becomes even more so at night. The streets come to life in an entirely different way, with music and laughter filling the air and the fragrance of fresh tapas wafting from packed bars. Seville understands how to do evenings properly. Whether you want to see an intimate flamenco show, go to a rooftop bar with a view, or take a calm stroll along the river, Seville has various options for evening entertainment. So, let's go to the center of Seville's dynamic nightlife, where I've spent many an evening taking up the enchantment of the city under the stars.

Flamenco Performances in the Heart of Seville

Flamenco in Seville is more than simply a show; it's an emotional rollercoaster involving music, dance, and raw passion. I remember my first flamenco show like it was yesterday. I'd heard and read about it, but nothing prepared me for the intensity of being there, in the middle of the performance. The quick claps, the screaming of the guitar, the rhythmic stomps of the dancers—it all engulfed me like a tornado. This was not a performance; it was a conversation between the artists and their audience, and I was fortunate to be a part of it.

La Carbonería is a must-visit. It's concealed down a narrow alley in the Santa Cruz district, and you could pass right past it without knowing what's inside. The setting is basic, almost rustic, with wooden benches and soft lighting that creates the ideal atmosphere. What distinguishes it is its authenticity; this is no tourist trap. The performers are exceptional, putting their heart and energy into each song and dance. The enthusiasm is strong, and it feels as if you're experiencing something absolutely unique.

El Arenal is another popular place for high-quality flamenco. Located near the river, this establishment provides a slightly more polished experience while retaining the raw intensity that defines flamenco. The performers here are among the greatest in Seville, and you will leave with a strong admiration for the art form. It's more of a dinner-and-show experience, so come hungry—you'll be treated to some delicious Andalusian cuisine as well.

Flamenco is so popular in Seville that it may be found almost anywhere. Flamenco will captivate you whether you visit a well-known location or a small pub with impromptu performances. Just make sure you don't sit too close to the front—I've discovered the hard way that the emotion in the artists' stomps may occasionally be felt (literally) in the shape of flying shoes!

Rooftop Bars with Breathtaking Views

As the sun sets over Seville and the warm glow of twilight takes over, there's no better place to be than on a rooftop bar with a drink in hand. Seville's rooftop bars provide the ideal balance of relaxation and panoramic views, and there's nothing better than enjoying a cocktail while admiring the breathtaking metropolis.

The EME Catedral Hotel's rooftop bar is one of my personal favorite spots. It's just a few steps from the church, and the view of the Giralda from above is breathtaking. The tower stands tall and beautiful, lighted against the night sky, and you can almost feel the history flowing from it. The bar itself is sleek and beautiful, with comfortable seating and a wide variety of beverages. Whether you want a basic Mojito or something more experimental, this restaurant provides. Trust me: once you've seen the view from here, every other rooftop bar will pale in comparison.

La Terraza de Doña María, located on top of the Hotel Doña María, is also a good alternative. It's a more laid-back atmosphere, ideal for nights when you just want to rest and unwind. The view is spectacular—again, the Giralda steals the show—but the attitude is more informal, with comfy seats and a welcoming setting. It's the ideal place to relax with a glass of vino tinto while watching the city lights glitter in the background.

For a more authentic experience, visit La Terraza del Cristina, which is a little off the main road but well worth the trip. It is positioned above the Hotel Cristina and provides beautiful views of the Guadalquivir River and Triana region. This location feels less touristy, and you'll be surrounded by people having a calm evening with a bottle of wine. It's a small bit of heaven, and the river breeze makes it ideal on a hot summer night.

Night Strolls Along the Guadalquivir

A moonlight stroll along the Guadalquivir River is ideal for those seeking solitude and quiet. After midnight, the riverbank takes on a whole different mood, with city lights reflecting off the water and soothing sounds of laughter and music flowing through the air. It's one of my favorite ways to unwind after a long day.

Begin your trek near the Torre del Oro, which is magnificently lit at night. The tower has stood watch over the river since the 13th century, and it looks much more spectacular at night. From there, follow the river, passing by the majestic Palacio de San Telmo and the vibrant Triana Bridge.

As you walk, you'll notice couples sitting on the riverside, sipping a bottle of wine or engaging in calm conversation. The riverfront is a favorite destination for both locals and tourists, and there's something relaxing about being near the water as the city hums softly in the background. I like to grab an ice cream from one of the sellers along the route and meander about, taking in the atmosphere.

Explore this bustling area at night by crossing Trianavia via the Puente de Isabel II. The streets are bustling with activity, and there are numerous bars and cafes where you can grab a drink. The view of Seville's skyline from Triana is stunning, especially with the Giralda and Alcázar shining in the background. It's the ideal way to end a quiet evening, with the city lights glinting on the sea.

Traditional Sevillian Tapas Bars

Eating tapas in Seville is virtually a sport, and I'm always keen to take part. The city's tapas bars are famed, and there's no better way to spend an evening than going from one to the next, eating new foods and taking in the bustling environment. Tapas culture in

Seville is all on sharing, so gather some pals and prepare to feast.

One of my top recommendations is El Rinconcillo, Seville's oldest tapas bar, which dates back to 1670. Walking into this establishment feels like stepping back in time, with its dark wooden beams and walls stocked with sherry bottles. The bartenders make speedy recommendations, and the espinacas with garbanzos (spinach with chickpeas) is a must-try. Grab a seat at the bar if possible—watching the bartenders scribble your bill in chalk on the tabletop is all part of the experience.

Another favorite of mine is Bodega Santa Cruz, which is located close the church. This bustling tavern is always full, but don't let that discourage you from ordering some of their famed montaditos (little sandwiches) and tortilla de camarones (shrimp fritters). The loudness and excitement here are contagious, and before you know it, you'll be mingling with locals and toasting strangers.

For something a little more modern, try La Azotea, a contemporary tapas bar with a unique cuisine. Their tuna tartare and hog cheeks in red wine sauce are popular dishes, and the atmosphere is upmarket without being pretentious. It's an excellent place to begin your tapas crawl before going on to more conventional establishments.

Pace yourself when eating tapas in Seville—there are so many things to taste, and you don't want to fill up too quickly. Order a few plates at each bar, share them with your buddies, and then move on to the next location. Don't forget to wash it all down with a glass of Manzanilla or tinto de verano!

Live Music Venues and Local Nightlife

If you enjoy music, Seville will not disappoint. The city boasts a thriving live music culture, with venues ranging from intimate jazz cafes to raucous nightclubs. There's something for everyone, whether you want to relax with some jazz or dance the night away.

Jazz Naimai is one of the city's most popular live jazz venues. Tucked away in the Alameda de Hércules area, this modest pub has a relaxing ambiance and hosts local jazz performers most nights of the week. The music is always excellent, and the crowd is a mix of locals and tourists who have come to enjoy the relaxing music. It's the ideal place to spend a nice night out with friends, sipping wine and listening to music.

Sala X, a prominent live music venue that presents a variety of genres ranging from indie rock to electronic music, is a good place to go for something more energetic. The crowd here is youthful and energetic, and the atmosphere is always exciting. I once strayed into a local band's concert and ended up staying until the early morning, dancing and singing along with the crowd. It's the type of location where anything can happen, and it's always a wonderful time.

If dancing is more your thing, check out Uthopia or Groucho, two of Seville's best nightclubs. The music is loud, the drinks are plentiful, and the dance floors are crowded. It's a terrific way to unwind and dance the night away while taking in Seville's bustling nightlife.

Theaters and Cultural Performances

Seville's cultural scene goes much beyond flamenco and live music. The city is home to several stunning theatres that showcase a range of acts, including opera, ballet, and modern dance.

The Teatro de la Maestranza is Seville's main performing arts theater, and seeing a show there is a must for any culture fan. The theatre is set on the banks of the Guadalquivir, and its breathtaking architecture is complemented by world-class performances inside. Whether you're attending an opera, ballet, or classical music, you're in for an incredible experience.

For a more personal experience, visit Teatro Lope de Vega, a smaller venue that holds a variety of entertainment such as plays, concerts, and dance shows. The theatre itself is a work of art, with its gorgeous design and comfortable seating. I once saw a contemporary dance performance here, and the intimate setting made me feel like I was a part of the show.

If you're looking for something unusual and entertaining, visit the Alameda de Hércules district, which is home to a variety of street performers, open-air events, and smaller theatre facilities that give one-of-a-kind performances. It's an excellent way to explore Seville's creative spirit in a more relaxed setting.

Whether you're seeing a passionate flamenco show, drinking a cocktail with a view of the Giralda, or dancing the night away in one of Seville's vibrant clubs, the city has infinite options for nighttime entertainment. Seville comes alive after dark, and there's always something fresh and fascinating to find. So grab your buddies, hit the town, and get ready for an unforgettable night in Seville—the evenings are where the magic happens.

Chapter 7

EXPLORING THE NEIGHBORHOODS

One of my favorite things about Seville is how it feels like a metropolis made up of many villages, each with its own personality, idiosyncrasies, and rhythms. You can travel a few blocks and be transported to an entirely other world—one moment you're surrounded by the winding, old alleyways of Santa Cruz, the next you're in the midst of Nervión's sophisticated commercial district. Seville's districts are both different and lovely, and each one provides a distinct glimpse into Sevillian life. Allow me to take you on a tour of some of my favorite districts, where I've gotten lost, joked with locals, and discovered the true essence of this city.

Santa Cruz: The Historical Jewish Quarter

Santa Cruz is the neighborhood where Seville shows off its most romantic and mysterious side. The city's old Jewish quarter is a network of narrow lanes and secret plazas that feels right out of a storybook. I've been through Santa Cruz more times than I can count, and I still get lost in its winding alleys—but that's part of the appeal. There's always something new to uncover, whether it's a small, flower-filled patio or a centuries-old fountain that trickles gently in a hidden corner.

One of my favorite spots in Santa Cruz is the Plaza de los Venerables, a little square surrounded by whitewashed buildings and orange trees. It's one of those locations where time appears to slow down. I enjoy sitting at a café here, sipping a café con leche, and people-watching while the world moves slowly around me. The Hospital de los Venerables, located on the square, is a lovely 17th-century edifice that today houses an art center, with a calm courtyard that is ideal for some introspection.

Santa Cruz is also home to some of Seville's most recognizable landmarks, such as the Alcázar and the Seville Cathedral, making it impossible to go more than a few meters without coming across a piece of history. Even beyond the major attractions, it is the minor elements that distinguish Santa Cruz—the azulejos (colorful ceramic tiles) on the walls, the perfume of jasmine in the air, and the echo of footsteps on the cobblestones. It's a neighborhood designed for exploration, and getting lost is the greatest way to discover its magic.

Triana: The Birthplace of Flamenco

Across the Puente de Triana, you'll find Triana, a distinct community. Triana feels like a universe separate from the rest of Seville; it's grungy, real, and full of character. Flamenco originated here, and the spirit of the dance pervades the neighborhood. It's in the air and the way things go here. I've spent many evenings meandering through Triana, listening to the faint strumming of guitars coming from open windows and watching impromptu flamenco performances in tiny, dimly lit pubs.

Triana is well-known for its ceramics, with shops along Calle Alfarería specializing in hand-painted tiles. I remember visiting Cerámica Santa Ana, one of Triana's oldest workshops, and being captivated by the craftsmen' talent and precision as they painted elaborate motifs on the tiles. If you want a keepsake that embodies the essence of Seville, here is the place to go.

One of my favorite places in Triana is the Mercado de Triana, a lively market near the bridge. This market is a sensory feast, with vividly colored fruits and vegetables heaped high, the aroma of fresh seafood, and the noise of blades as butchers carve meat. It's the ideal place to get a bite to eat, whether you're craving jamón ibérico or freshly shucked oysters. And don't skip out on the small tapas stalls—order a platter of pimientos de padrón and a glass of fino to feel like a true Trianero.

Arenal, Seville's Bullfighting District

The Arenal area is associated with one of Spain's most renowned (and controversial) traditions: bullfighting. This region is home to Seville's famed bullring, Plaza de Toros de la Maestranza, one of Spain's oldest and most prestigious. Whether or not you enjoy bullfighting, Arenal's history and culture are firmly rooted, and the place exudes gravitas.

I recall visiting the Museo Taurino, which is located inside the bullring, and being astonished by the extensive history on display. From the extravagant matador costumes to the paintings depicting legendary battles, the museum provides an intriguing peek into the world of bullfighting. Even if you don't want to watch a fight (which is understandable— bullfighting isn't for everyone), the museum is worth a visit for the cultural insights it offers.

Aside from bullfighting, Arenal is a dynamic area with a lot to offer. The streets are dotted with tapas bars and restaurants, and it's one of the best places in town to sample some of Seville's famous seafood. La Islais is a personal favorite of mine—this unassuming little eatery delivers some of the city's freshest seafood, and their gambas al ajillo (garlic shrimp) is to die for. After a meal here, I prefer to go along the Paseo de Cristóbal Colón, which runs alongside the river and provides beautiful views of the Torre del Oro.

Alameda: A Hip & Bohemian Vibe

For an entirely different vibe, visit Alameda de Hércules, Seville's fashionable, bohemian area. Alameda is one of Seville's most colorful and vibrant neighborhoods, attracting the city's creative types, including painters, musicians, and writers. The Plaza de la Alameda, a large area dotted with bars, cafes, and odd stores, serves as the neighborhood's core. It's a terrific area to people-watch, especially in the evening when the square is crowded with residents enjoying a drink or two.

I've spent many evenings in Alameda, bouncing from one bar to the next, trying artisan beers and tapas and taking in the laid-back vibe. Al Aljibeis is one of my favorite restaurants—this stylish eatery serves wonderful modern tapas with a twist, and their rooftop terrace is the ideal place to dine on a nice evening. Casa Paco is a local institution noted for its affordable beverages and lively environment.

Alameda also has some of the city's top live music venues. FunClub is a small but iconic venue that features indie and rock bands from all over Spain, while Sala X is the place to go for electronic music or a DJ set. The nightlife in Alameda is vibrant and eclectic, and it's the type of neighborhood where you can dance till the early hours of the morning or simply relax with a drink and soak up the vibe.

Nervión: Modern Seville

While many of Seville's neighborhoods are rich in history, Nervión is all about modernism. This is the city's business area, which includes elegant office buildings, high-end shopping malls, and some of Seville's best modern architecture. Nervión is not the most scenic area of the city, but if you're looking for a change from the old-world beauty of Santa Cruz or Triana, it provides a unique experience.

One of Nervión's biggest attractions is Nervión Plaza, a large shopping mall ideal for some retail therapy. You'll discover a mix of international and local retailers, as well as a variety of restaurants and cafes to eat at. I once spent a full afternoon here, strolling through the stores and basking in the air conditioning (a godsend in Seville's summer heat).

Nervión is also home to Sevilla FC's stadium, Estadio Ramón Sánchez-Pizjuán, which is a must-see for every football enthusiast. The atmosphere is electrifying, and even if you aren't a die-hard fan, the enthusiasm of the locals is inspiring. I once went to a match and by the conclusion, I was cheering and chanting with the crowd, despite the fact that I had no idea what was going on half of the time.

Macarena: Rich in Tradition and Culture

Finally, there is Macarena, a neighborhood steeped in tradition and culture. This region is a little off the usual route, but it's one of the most authentic portions of Seville, and it's definitely worth a visit. Macarena is well known for the Basilica de la Macarena, which houses the renowned Virgen de la Macarena, a statue of the Virgin Mary that occupies a special place in the hearts of many Sevillanos. During Semana Santa (Holy Week), the statue is paraded through the streets of Seville, making it one of the most emotional and significant events of the year.

The Basilica is a magnificent example of Baroque architecture, with its golden altar and beautifully painted interior. I went during a quieter period, and the tranquility of the basilica was a pleasant relief from the city's rush and bustle. The inhabitants' devotion to the Virgin of La Macarena is

The reverence in the air is evident, and even if you are not religious, you cannot help but feel moved.

Macarena also houses Las Setas, a huge wooden structure formally known as the Metropol Parasol. This modern architectural marvel is the world's largest wooden building, with breathtaking panoramic views of Seville from its rooftop walkway. It's a bit of a departure from the traditional feel of the rest of the neighborhood, but that's what makes Macarena so appealing—it's a location where the old and new coexist in perfect harmony.

Each of Seville's neighborhoods provides a unique perspective on the city's culture, history, and way of life. Whether you're lost in the meandering lanes of Santa Cruz, soaking up the artistic energy of Alameda, or discovering Nervión's modern side, there's always something new to discover. Seville is a city of contrasts, and its neighborhoods reflect its diversified and energetic nature. So, put on your walking shoes, get a map (or don't—getting lost is half the fun), and go out to discover the many facets of this magnificent city.

Chapter 8

SEVILLE'S FESTIVALS AND EVENTS

If there's one thing you should know about Seville, it's that it's not afraid to celebrate. In reality, it appears like there is always something going on, ranging from enormous religious processions to bustling festivals and even more modest cultural events. The Sevillanos know how to enjoy life, and their festivals demonstrate this. During my time in Seville, I had the opportunity to attend several of the city's most well-known festivals, and believe me when I say that Seville knows how to throw a party like no other.

Let's look at some of Seville's most famous festivals and events, where history meets spectacle and the city comes alive with color, music, and joy.

Semana Santa (Holy Week)

Let's begin with Semana Santa, or Holy Week, which is undoubtedly Seville's most well-known and deeply ingrained event. If you visit Seville during Holy Week, you will not only see the city, but also feel it. The entire atmosphere shifts, and it's impossible not to be caught up in the enthusiasm and dedication that fills the streets.

During Semana Santa, Seville offers some of the most magnificent and dramatic processions you've ever seen. These processions include pasos, which are large, ornate floats holding religious sculptures depicting scenes from the Passion of Christ. Each paso is borne by costaleros (guys who walk beneath the floats and bear their enormous weight on their necks and shoulders). I will never forget seeing a paso for the first time, as it moved slowly through the streets, swaying slightly, with the costaleros hidden beneath, their strength and determination unseen but apparent.

What struck me the most was the absolute reverence of it all. The streets were busy, but the silence was almost frightening. Then, out of nowhere, someone in the audience would start singing a saeta—a mournful, impromptu flamenco-style song aimed at the Virgin Mary—and you could feel the hairs on your arms stand up. Even if you are not religious, the experience is deeply compelling.

The most famous processions occur in the early hours of Madrugá, the night between Holy Thursday and Good Friday, when the most venerated pasos, such as the Virgen de la Macarena, pass through the city. Don't be shocked if you find yourself standing in the streets after midnight, shoulder to shoulder with Sevillanos who have been attending these processions since they were children. Semana Santa is an emotional rollercoaster that must be experienced firsthand to really understand.

Feria de Abril: The Spring Fair

After the seriousness of Semana Santa, Seville swings gears significantly for the Feria de Abril, the city's most colorful and lavish event. Consider this: thousands of brightly colored tents (or casetas) fill the Real de la Feria, a massive fairground on the outskirts of the city, and Sevillanos, dressed to the nines in traditional flamenco and corto trajes, come out to dance, drink, and socialize until the early hours of morning.

I got the opportunity to attend the Feria one year and felt as if I had been transported to another world. The streets are lined with horse-drawn carriages, the women wear exquisite flamenco costumes with frills that appear to stretch on forever, and the men wear wide-brimmed hats and crisp suits. Color, music, and a sense of pure delight may be found everywhere you look. If there is ever a time to celebrate Sevillian culture, it is during Feria.

The casetas are private tents where families, friends, and companies can eat, drink, and dance sevillanas (a traditional flamenco-style dance with a more celebratory feel). If you're lucky enough to be asked to one, consider it a sign that you've been welcomed by Sevillian society. If not, don't worry—there are plenty of public casetas where you can join in the fun, dance till your feet ache, and eat endless plates of jamón, tortilla de patatas, and rebujito (a delightful combination of manzanilla sherry and soda).

One thing I rapidly realized was that Feria is a marathon, not a sprint. The party lasts six days and does not actually begin until late afternoon, when the sun starts to set. Pace yourself, enjoy the ambiance, and, if possible, practice your sevillanas—you'll want to join the dance floor at least once!

Seville European Film Festival

While Seville is well-known for its traditional festivals, it also has a modern, artistic side that should be explored, particularly during the Seville European Film Festival. This festival, which takes place every November, celebrates European cinema and has grown into a major event for filmmakers, critics, and moviegoers from all over the continent.

I attended the festival one year and was astounded by the diversity of films on offer. From gritty indie films to big-budget movies, there's something for every kind of cinephile. Many of the screenings take place at the gorgeous Teatro Lope de Vega, a historic theatre that lends an air of old-world beauty to the modern films on display.

What I appreciate most about the Seville European Film Festival is that it is not limited to industry insiders. Many of the screenings are available to the public, and tickets are surprisingly inexpensive. It's an excellent opportunity to view a film that you might not see anywhere else and to witness the ingenuity and brilliance of European filmmakers. In addition, the festival frequently hosts Q&A sessions with filmmakers and actors, providing a behind-the-scenes peek at the filmmaking process.

For cinema fans, this festival is a hidden jewel in Seville's cultural calendar, and it's a terrific way to see the city in a new light—one in which art and creativity take center stage.

Corpus Christi Celebrations

Seville is no stranger to religious events, and Corpus Christi is another occasion that highlights the city's strong Catholic roots. Corpus Christi, held 60 days after Easter, is a magnificent procession through Seville's streets, with the Giralda and Cathedral as backdrops.

While not as passionate or emotional as Semana Santa, Corpus Christi has its own distinct appeal. The streets are decorated with magnificent altars, flowers, and tapestries, and the procession features some of the city's most prominent religious personalities and relics. One of the attractions is the Custodia de Arfe, a giant silver monstrance carried through the streets and glistening in the sun.

What I appreciate most about Corpus Christi is the celebratory spirit that pervades the city. It's a time for families to gather together, for kids to dress up in their best clothes, and for the community to celebrate its beliefs and customs. There is a sense of pride in the air, and even if you are not religious, it is difficult not to be carried away by the beauty and history of it all.

Following the parade, the streets are packed with residents enjoying a drink or two at their favorite tabernas, and it's the ideal time to join in the celebration, whether you're sipping wine or eating a platter of churros con chocolate.

Bienal de Flamenco: A Flamenco Extravaganza

If you enjoy flamenco (and who doesn't after visiting Seville?), the Bienal de Flamenco is a must-see event. Every two years, this month-long event celebrates everything flamenco, bringing together the world's top dancers, singers, and musicians.

I went to the Bienal one year, and it was a life-changing experience. Flamenco is more than just a dance or a song; it's an art form that expresses the deepest emotions, and the Bienal showcases flamenco at its pinnacle. The performances take place in some of Seville's most renowned venues, including the Teatro de la Maestranza and the small Casa de la Memoria, and each one is a masterclass in emotion, technique, and talent.

What I enjoy about the Bienal is that it has something for everyone. If you're a traditionalist, there are plenty of vintage flamenco performances that highlight the art form's roots. If you prefer contemporary interpretations, there are avant-garde performances that push the boundaries of flamenco, incorporating elements of jazz, modern dance, and even hip-hop.

The energy during the Bienal is intoxicating, and by the end, you'll feel ready to join your own flamenco group (albeit my attempts at flamenco footwork were more funny than graceful).

Christmas Markets and Festivities

Seville may not be a snowy winter wonderland, but it more than compensates with its Christmas markets and festive atmosphere. I spent one Christmas season in Seville, and it was one of the most magical times of year. The city is decked out in lights, the air is thick with the aroma of roasted chestnuts, and Christmas carols reverberate through the streets.

The Feria del Belén, a Christmas market solely dedicated to nativity scenes, is one of the holiday season's highlights. This market, located near the Cathedral, has hundreds of shops selling everything you could possible need to make your own nativity scene, from tiny miniatures of the Holy Family to beautifully crafted

Buildings and animals. Even if you don't intend to create your own belén, it's worth a visit just to admire the beauty and detail that goes into these miniature marvels.

There are also numerous additional Christmas markets across the city where you can buy handmade gifts, drink hot chocolate, and eat traditional Spanish sweets such as turrón and polvorones. The Mercado de Navidad de la Alameda, in the Alameda de Hércules area, is one of my favorite Christmas markets. It's a little more unconventional, with vendors selling unique, locally made crafts and art, and the atmosphere is bright and celebratory.

Carnival in Seville

Last but not least, let's discuss Carnival. While Seville's Carnival is not as well-known as those in Cadiz or Rio de Janeiro, it is nonetheless a vibrant and colorful event that fills the city's streets. Carnival takes place in the weeks preceding Lent and is all about having fun before the solemnity of the Lenten season begins.

Sevillanos parade through the streets in elaborate costumes, and the city is alive with parades, live music, and plenty of partying. The Gran Cabalgata, a gigantic procession through the city with floats, dancers, and musicians, is one of Carnival's highlights. I went to the parade one year and became engrossed in the celebratory mood, surrounded by individuals dressed in everything from flamenco gowns to pirate garb.

While Carnival in Seville may not have the crazy reputation of other cities, it is nevertheless an excellent opportunity to explore the whimsical and fun-loving side of Sevillian culture. And, of course, a Spanish festival would be incomplete without plenty of food and drink, so expect to see a plethora of street vendors offering everything from churros to empanadas, as well as plenty of opportunities to raise a glass of sherry to the festivities.

Seville's festivals and events provide a glimpse into the city's essence, where tradition, culture, and festivity blend seamlessly. Whether you're watching the solemn processions of Semana Santa, dancing the night away at the Feria de Abril, or immersed in the flamenco magic of the Bienal, Seville's festivals are unforgettable. So mark your calendars, reserve your tickets, and prepare to rejoice—because there is always something to celebrate in Seville.

Chapter 9

DAYTRIPS FROM SEVILLE

Seville, as engaging as it is, is an excellent starting point for touring some of Spain's most beautiful and historically significant sites. I've had the pleasure of taking a few amazing day trips from the city, and each one felt like uncovering another layer of Andalusia's rich cultural and environmental fabric. From ancient Roman ruins to sherry-sipping sessions in sun-soaked vineyards, these day outings provide a welcome respite from Seville's hectic streets. So, if you want to go beyond the city's lovely bounds, buckle up! Here are six day trips from Seville that will transport you to a world of history, beauty, and the perfect amount of adventure.

Córdoba: The Mesmerising Mosque-Cathedral

When it comes to day travels from Seville, Córdoba frequently tops the list—and with good reason. This historic city is home to one of the most astonishing architectural marvels I've ever seen: the Córdoba Mosque-Cathedral. My mouth dropped to the floor the first time I went inside. Consider this: a vast forest of red and white striped arches reaching eternally in all directions, illuminated by gentle golden light streaming through elegant windows. It's the type of setting that makes you feel as if you've stepped into another dimension—one where time has no meaning and history unfolds around you.

The Mezquita is a remarkable example of Islamic construction, but what truly distinguishes it is that a cathedral was built in the center of the mosque during the Christian reconquest. It's as if two universes collided and agreed to cohabit, although uneasily. Walking inside the Mezquita, I was astonished by how smoothly the two religions' architectural styles merged, although each element remained distinct. One moment you're standing beneath an elaborate mihrab (a prayer niche facing Mecca), the next you're looking up at soaring Gothic arches and Christian altarpieces. It's a mind-bending encounter that makes you wonder what else Córdoba has in store.

Beyond the Mezquita, Córdoba is a beautiful city to visit. The Jewish Quarter is filled with narrow, twisting lanes, lovely patios full with flowers, and modest artisan shops selling hand-painted ceramics and silver jewelry. And don't get me started on the food—Córdoba is the birthplace of salmorejo, a richer, creamier cousin of gazpacho, which I highly recommend sampling at one of the many outdoor cafes that line the streets.

Jerez de la Frontera: Sherry and Horses

If you want fine beverages, beautiful horses, and a touch of old-world elegance, Jerez de la Frontera should be on your list of day trip destinations from Seville. Jerez is the birthplace of sherry, so you can't go without trying some of the local types. I'm not going to lie: before my trip to Jerez, I believed sherry was something my grandmother drank at Christmas. But after a day spent touring the bodegas (wineries) and sampling everything from finoto to oloroso, I was a different person.

Bodegas Tío Pepe is a well-known sherry house in Jerez. Visitors can enjoy a guided tour of the centuries-old vaults, learn about the sherry-making process, and sample a glass or two. The trip concludes with a large tasting session, and by the conclusion, I was sure that sherry is the world's most undervalued drink.

But Jerez is more than simply sherry. The city is also known for its Andalusian horses, and if you arrange your visit correctly, you may see a performance at the

Royal Andalusian School of Equestrian Art. Watching these gorgeous horses perform sophisticated dressage routines to classical music is just amazing. The horses appear to glide over the arena, with movements so fluid and elegant that it's difficult to believe they're genuine. Even if you aren't a horse fan, this event is a must-see—it's like seeing poetry in motion.

Carmona's Ancient Roman Roots

Carmona is the perfect day trip for those who want to feel like they've stepped back in time. This modest town, just a short drive from Seville, is rich in history, from the old Roman necropolis to the majestic Alcázar. Carmona is like Seville's quieter, more introspective cousin—it's just as lovely, but with fewer tourists and a slower pace of life.

The Roman Necropolis, a historic burial cemetery dating back to the first century, is a must-see for anybody visiting Carmona. Walking around the ruins, one can't help but admire the exquisite tombs and the sense of history that pervades the atmosphere. It's a hauntingly beautiful spot, and as I stood there surrounded by old tombs, I couldn't help but imagine the lives of the people who used to live here.

Carmona's Alcázar de la Puerta de Sevilla is another must-see. This stronghold has guarded the town for generations, and the top of the tower offers panoramic views of the surrounding landscape. It's the ideal place to enjoy the beauty of Andalusia's rolling hills and olive trees while learning about the town's rich history.

After a day of touring, visit Plaza San Fernando, Carmona's picturesque main plaza, and unwind at one of the outdoor cafes with a cool cerveza and some tapas. Carmona's slower pace of life is contagious, and you'll find yourself relishing every second of this quiet, historically significant town.

Doñana National Park: A Nature Reserve

Doñana National Park is a must-see destination for nature lovers. This UNESCO World Heritage Site is one of Europe's most important wetlands, home to a diverse range of animals, including flamingos, imperial eagles, and the rare Iberian lynx. Exploring Doñana was a dream come true for me as a wildlife enthusiast.

A guided 4x4 safari is one of the greatest ways to explore the park. The park's topography is quite diversified, ranging from marshlands and sand dunes to deep pine woods and scrubland. As we bounced around the dirt trails, our guide pointed out various bird and animal species, and I was continually eyeing the horizon for a sight of the Iberian lynx (spoiler: they're quite elusive, and I didn't see one). Nonetheless, being surrounded by such unspoiled environment was invigorating, and the sheer diversity of birdlife made the journey worthwhile.

For a more relaxing experience, you can tour the park by boat. A boat journey down the Guadalquivir River provides a unique view of Doñana's marshes and bird life. There's something really calm about gliding along the river, surrounded by nature, with only the sounds of birds and the smooth lapping of water against the boat.

Ronda: A Breathtaking Cliffside Town

If you want to go on a day excursion that will literally steal your breath away, Ronda is the place to be. This cliffside village, poised spectacularly above the El Tajo Gorge, is one of the most picturesque sites I've ever seen. When I first saw Ronda's famed Puente Nuevo (New Bridge) across the gorge, I couldn't help but gasp. The tremendous plunge from the bridge to the river below is dizzying, but what about the views? It is absolutely worthwhile.

Ronda has a long and interesting history. It's one of Spain's oldest towns, dating back to the Celts, Romans, and Moors. Walking around the old town, you'll see a combination of Moorish architecture, traditional Spanish whitewashed houses, and picturesque cobblestone streets. One of the highlights is the Palacio de Mondragón, a gorgeous Moorish palace with lovely gardens and breathtaking views of the gorge.

For a true experience of Ronda, head to the Plaza de Toros, one of Spain's oldest bullrings. Even if bullfighting isn't your thing, the museum within provides an intriguing look into the history and culture of this contentious sport. Furthermore, being in the midst of the bullring and picturing the thousands of fans who previously packed the stands is a moving experience.

But, for me, Ronda's true magic is in its natural beauty. After touring the town, I enjoy having a leisurely walk into the countryside, which offers panoramic views of the neighboring mountains and valleys. It's the kind of place that makes you want to stop, breathe, and soak it all in.

Cádiz: Spain's Oldest City

Last but not least, we have Cádiz, which is known as Spain's oldest city. Cádiz, located on a short strip of land that juts out into the Atlantic Ocean, is a city rich in nautical history and sun-soaked charm. I've always been drawn to coastal cities, and Cádiz has a unique enchantment that's difficult to describe.

One of the greatest ways to discover Cádiz is to simply meander around its narrow streets, becoming lost in the maze of historic buildings, churches, and plazas. The Cathedral of Cádizis is a must.

Visit, with its golden dome sparkling in the sun and magnificent views of the city from its bell tower. I recall hiking to the top of the tower and being welcomed by the view of the Atlantic stretching out eternally before me, with the city's whitewashed houses gathered below. It's a view that will stick with you long after you leave.

Cádiz is also known for its vibrant Carnival celebrations, which are among the largest and most extravagant in Spain. If you are fortunate enough to visit during Carnival season, you will be treated to street parades, flashy costumes, and nonstop partying that lasts far into the night.

And, of course, no trip to Cádiz is complete without a visit to the beach. The city's beaches are some of the greatest in Andalusia, with La Caleta Beach being my particular favorite. It's a little, crescent-shaped beach situated between two ancient fortresses, and lying on the sand while watching the boats bobbing gently in the harbor is wonderfully calming.

Whether you're experiencing the ancient history of Córdoba, sipping sherry in Jerez, or admiring the natural beauty of Ronda, Seville's surroundings provide a plethora of fascinating experiences. Each day trip takes you on a tour of Andalusia's rich history, breathtaking scenery, and vibrant culture. So pack your day bag, board a train or rent a car, and prepare to see the delights that lie just beyond Seville's city limits.

Chapter 10

SEVILLE'S CULINARY DELIGHTS

Seville is a city that celebrates life, and nowhere is this more apparent than in its cuisine. The seductive aroma of grilled meats, fresh seafood, and frying garlic entices you from the moment you walk in. Whether you're eating tapas in a crowded bar, experiencing street cuisine at one of the city's many markets, or relaxing with a dinner in a historic square, Seville's culinary culture will leave you both satiated and wanting more. As someone who has spent many enjoyable afternoons and evenings eating my way through this city, I can certainly state that Seville's food is more than simply a requirement; it's an experience.

Allow me to take you on a delightful voyage through Seville's gastronomic wonders, complete with a few recommendations, a dash of comedy, and some insider information.

Tapas 101: What to Order?

First things first, let's speak tapas. If you've heard anything about Spanish cuisine, you've probably heard of tapas. Tapas are a way of life in Seville, and while I used to think of them as "appetizers," I soon realized they are so much more. Tapas are a social event, a reason to get together with friends, and an excuse to stay out a little later.

Walking into a tapas bar might be daunting. The menu appears to be limitless, with options ranging from grilled prawns to fried squid and ham croquettes. Don't even get me started on the various types of jamón (cured ham). But don't worry, I've already done the hard work (read: considerable eating) for you. Here are five must-try tapas to help you get started:

- Tortilla de Patatas: This is Spain's take on a potato omelette, and it's a classic for good reason. It's fluffy, flavorful, and ideal for soaking up any wine or sherry you might be drinking. Every bar claims to create the best tortilla, and they all taste great.

- Gambas al Ajillo: If you enjoy garlic (and who doesn't?), this meal of prawns sautéed in garlic and olive oil will become your best buddy. The sizzling prawns are presented in a little, bubbling dish of oil, which is ideal for dipping bread into afterward.

- Solomillo al Whiskey: Pork tenderloin in a whiskey sauce may seem like a weird combination, but believe me, it works. The whiskey imparts a smokey sweetness to the perfectly cooked pork, and it's one of those dishes that leaves you wondering why more things aren't made with whiskey.

- Jamón Ibérico: This is the highlight of any tapas meal. Jamón ibérico, made from acorn-fed pigs, is melt-in-your-mouth wonderful. You can find it hanging in practically every pub, thinly sliced and presented on a dish with nothing but its own perfection.

- Croquetas: These deep-fried balls of creamy béchamel sauce packed with ham, chicken, or cod are a true comfort meal. I've been known to consume an embarrassing amount of croquetas in one sitting.

The beauty of tapas is that they are designed to be shared. Order a couple plates, get a drink, and enjoy the flavors of Seville. And if you're feeling experimental, don't be afraid to ask the bartender for a recommendation—they always seem to know just what you need.

Must-Try Dishes in Seville

Beyond tapas, there are specific meals in Seville that you must try. These dishes are part of the city's culinary DNA and provide a deeper look into Andalusian cuisine.

Salmorejo is one of the most iconic foods. This chilled tomato soup is a cousin of gazpacho, but it's thicker, creamier, and more luxurious. It's made with ripe tomatoes, bread, olive oil, and garlic, and is typically topped with a chopped hard-boiled egg and diced jamón. On a hot day (which is most days in Seville), a bowl of salmorejo feels like a refreshing, savory hug. Pair it with a glass of crisp fino (dry sherry) for the ultimate supper.

For seafood enthusiasts, Pescaito Frito (fried fish) is a must. The fish is gently battered and cooked to golden perfection, served with nothing but a wedge of lemon. It's easy, but the quality of the fish and the ability to fry it make all the difference. For the greatest pescaito, go to Triana; it's available at practically every bar along the river.

If you have a large appetite, you should have Carrillada de Cerdo. This dish of slow-cooked pig cheeks is so delicate that it almost falls apart with a fork. The cheeks are cooked in a rich red wine sauce until they're melt-in-your-mouth tender, and they're typically served with patatas fritas (fried potatoes) or mashed potatoes to soak up the sauce.

Finally, do not leave Seville without trying Huevos a la Flamenca. This classic cuisine is a baked casserole of eggs, chorizo, and veggies that is typically served sizzling hot in a clay dish. It's rustic, hearty, and full of flavor—ideal for a late breakfast or lunch.

Where To Eat Like A Local

One of the pleasures of dining in Seville is discovering hidden, locals-only restaurants that do not appear on TripAdvisor's top ten listings. Don't get me wrong, there are plenty of wonderful restaurants in the tourist areas, but for a more authentic experience, head to the neighborhoods where Sevillanos eat.

Blanca Paloma, a no-frills tapas tavern in Triana, is where people go to get their daily fix of croquetas, grilled fish, and stewed beef. The rates are reasonable, the portions are large, and the environment is lively and inviting.

For a taste of history, visit El Rinconcillo, Seville's oldest tapas tavern, which dates back to 1670. Walking into this establishment feels like going back in time, with dark wooden beams and bartenders penning your tab in chalk on the bar. The espinacas with garbanzos (spinach with chickpeas) here is legendary, and it's often busy with a mix of locals and knowledgeable tourists.

If you're in the Alameda de Hércules district, stop by Duo Tapas, a modern spin on traditional tapas. This contemporary establishment serves unique cuisine with a twist, such as tuna tataki and small burgers, as well as classics like berenjenas con miel (fried eggplant with honey).

Finally, for a more private dining experience, visit La Azotea. With multiple locations throughout the city, this restaurant serves an upgraded version of tapas made with fresh, seasonal ingredients and a dash of culinary inventiveness. The pork cheeks in red wine are outstanding, and the setting is ideal for a relaxing evening meal.

Seville's Famous Food Markets

If you want to see Seville's food culture at its most alive, visit one of the city's food markets. These crowded markets are packed with local sellers offering everything from fresh fruit to cured meats, cheeses, and seafood. It's the ideal place to grab a snack, fill up on supplies, or simply stroll about and take in the sights and smells.

The Mercado de Triana is one of the city's most well-known markets, and it's a sensory experience. This market, located across the river from the city center, is a local tradition, with sellers selling everything from fresh seafood to jamón ibérico. The market also includes a few tiny bars and cafés where you can sit and eat tapas or drink wine. I've spent many mornings perusing the stalls, picking up fresh fruit and trying local cheeses.

Another excellent market is the Mercado de la Feria, which is located in the Ferian district. This market is little smaller and less popular than Mercado de Triana, yet it is just as attractive. It's the type of area where residents go to shop on a daily basis, and the atmosphere is always bustling. I recommend stopping by one of the stalls for a fresh bocadillo (sandwich) or a quick snack of crispy fried pork belly.

Wine and Sherry Tasting Tours

When it comes to drinking, Seville is famous for two things: wine and Sherry. While I've always enjoyed Spanish wines, it wasn't until I spent time in Seville that I really fell in love with sherry. This fortified wine, which may range from bone-dry to syrupy sweet, is a crucial ingredient of Andalusian cuisine, and Seville is the best place to learn about it.

A sherry tasting tour is one of the best ways to get acquainted with the world of sherry. Several bars and wine shops in Seville provide guided tastings, allowing you to try a variety of sherries while learning about the production process. La Carbonain Triana is one of my favorite venues for a sherry tasting—they have an excellent collection of sherries ranging from the light and dry fino to the deep and nutty oloroso. The skilled staff is passionate about sherry and will walk you through the several types, discussing the distinct flavors and how they match with food.

If you prefer wine, Seville is surrounded by some of the top wine-producing regions in Spain, and several

Companies provide day tours to surrounding wineries. I did a trip of the Montilla-Moriles region, which is a short drive from Seville, and it was a memorable experience. The sweeping vineyards, great hospitality, and, of course, wine made for an ideal day out. I returned with a renewed appreciation for Andalusian wines and a bottle or two to savor later.

Sweet Treats: Confectionery and Pastries

No lunch in Seville is complete without something sweet, and the city's bakeries and pastry stores are stocked with delectable sweets to satiate your sweet taste. Seville's candy, from torrijas to pestiños, is rich in heritage and offers a flavor of history with each bite.

Torrijas, a delicacy similar to French toast but somehow better, is one of my all-time favorites from Seville. Torrijas are slices of bread soaked with milk, sugar, and cinnamon, fried, then drizzled with honey or syrup. They're generally consumed during Semana Santa, but they're available all year at several of the city's bakeries. I recommend visiting Confitería La Campana, one of Seville's oldest and most beloved pastry shops, to enjoy their version.

Pestiños are a deep-fried pastry flavored with orange zest and honey. These small pieces of perfection are generally created around Christmas, but you can get them in bakeries all year. They're crispy, sweet, and dangerously addictive—I may have consumed an entire bag in one sitting once, but who's counting?

If you enjoy almonds, don't miss polvorones, a crumbly almond shortbread that melts in your mouth.

These are often linked with Christmas, although they are available year-round in Seville and make an excellent snack with a cup of coffee or tea.

Seville's culinary scene is a feast for the senses. Whether you're indulging in tapas, tasting local wines and sherries, or treating yourself to a delectable pastry, the city has countless possibilities to eat, drink, and be merry. So, pull up a chair, hoist a glass, and get ready to fall in love with Seville's flavors—just be prepared to relax your belt a little bit!

Chapter 11

THE HIDDEN GEMS OF SEVILLE

Seville is home to well-known attractions such as the Alcázar, Cathedral, and Giralda, but if you're anything like me, you'll find some of the city's lesser-known nooks to be equally (if not more) enchanting. While the huge monuments lure the tourists, the genuine spirit of Seville is frequently hidden in plain sight, waiting to be discovered by those who are willing to take a wrong turn, peep through a half-open door, or meander down a quiet alley. I've spent numerous days being delightfully lost in Seville, and I believe the city's spirit lives in its hidden treasures.

Here's a guide to Seville, which only those who take the time to investigate will discover—a city full of calm courtyards, enigmatic convents, and ancient wall ruins. These hidden gems may not be on the standard tourist itinerary, but believe me, they're worth the detour.

The Murillo Gardens

When I need a quiet moment away from Seville's bustling streets, I frequently go around the Murillo Gardens. These tranquil gardens, nestled immediately behind the Alcázar and the Barrio Santa Cruz, are a hidden gem that provides a respite in the middle of the city. The Murillo Gardens offer a more personal experience compared to the more popular Parque de María Luis.

These gardens, named after the famed Sevillian painter Bartolomé Esteban Murillo, commemorate the city's appreciation of art and environment. As you go around the paths, you'll observe a variety of fountains, sculptures, and brilliant flowerbeds that appear to bloom all year. The towering palms and orange trees give ample shade, making it ideal for a leisurely stroll, particularly in Seville's heat.

What I enjoy most about the Murillo Gardens is how they appear to invite you to slow down. It's a place where time seems to stop still, with only the sound of birds, the trickle of water from fountains, and the delicate rustle of leaves in the breeze. It's the perfect place to retreat with a good book or simply relax on a bench and take in the beauty of the city without being surrounded by tourists.

Convent of Santa Paula

Now here's a hidden gem that I nearly missed. The Convent of Santa Paula is not a well-known destination, yet it is a veritable treasure mine of history and traditions. Nestled in a peaceful nook of the Macarenaneighborhood, this 15th-century convent is still home to a community of nuns who create some of the best marmalades and preserves I've ever had.

Walking through the inconspicuous door, I felt transported to another period. The convent's cloisters are extremely serene, with arched hallways and a lovely center garden filled with flowers. But what truly distinguishes this location is the little museum within its walls, which has an outstanding collection of religious art, including pieces by Murillo and other Spanish masters.

The nuns' shop, where they sell their handcrafted sweets, was undoubtedly the highlight of my stay. I really recommend the orange marmalade—it's zesty, sweet, and bursting with the flavor of Seville's famed oranges. The experience of purchasing it through a revolving wooden door, where the nuns are hidden, added mystery and charm. It isn't every day that you obtain jam from a centuries-old monastery!

The Courtyards of Seville

Courtyards are what Seville excels at more than anywhere else. These calm, hidden oases, known as patios, are an important element of Sevillian life, providing a cool, shaded respite from the heat and a touch of nature in the heart of the city. The custom of the Sevillian courtyard extends back to Roman and Moorish times, and as you travel around the city, you'll frequently get glimpses of these private gardens through beautiful wrought-iron gates or open doors.

One of my favorite times of year to explore Seville's courtyards is during the annual Feria de los Patios, a celebration in which residents open up their private courtyards to the public. It's an opportunity to peep behind the doors of some of the city's most magnificent homes and see breathtaking patios adorned with flowers, fountains, and elaborate tilework. Even outside of the festival, Seville's courtyards are worth looking for.

One hidden gem I discovered was the Casa de Pilatos, a gorgeous palace with some of the most exquisite patios in the city. The blend of Renaissance and Mudejar architecture, with its cold marble columns, vivid azulejos (tiles), and lush flora, transports you to a fantasy. Each patio is like a small slice of paradise, and you could easily spend hours strolling through the palace, exploring new nooks and corners.

City's Old Walls

Seville's rich history is frequently concealed in plain sight, and one of the most fascinating vestiges of its past is the old city walls. These walls, originally constructed during the Roman era and then enlarged by the Moors, formerly encompassed the entire city, safeguarding it from attackers. While much of the wall has been lost to time, parts remain standing beautifully, quietly guarding Seville's past.

One of the best-preserved parts of the wall is located at the Macarena Gate, which was previously the city's northern entrance. The gate itself is stunning, painted in the brilliant yellow and white that are distinctive of Seville. Walking along the old walls, I couldn't help but think how life may have been centuries ago, when this wall would have served as the first line of defense against prospective threats.

The Basílica de la Macarena, located just beyond the Macarena Gate, houses the renowned Virgin of Hope of Macarena, a famous icon of Seville. If you're in the vicinity, stop by to visit the church and the iconic statue, which is essential to the city's Semana Santa procession.

The Dueñas Palace

The Palacio de las Dueñas, a lesser-known palace in Seville, is equally captivating as the Alcázar. This gorgeous 15th-century castle was formerly the home of the Duchess of Alba, one of Spain's most famous aristocrats, and it is a lovely blend of Gothic, Moorish, and Renaissance architecture.

As you wander through the palace's courtyards and gardens, you can't help but feel transported to another world. The environment is serene and intimate, and the buildings and rich vegetation give a sense of timeless elegance. The palace is rich with art and antiquities, many of which were collected by the Duchess herself, and roaming through the rooms gives you a sense of the history and grandeur that once existed within these walls.

One of the palace's most notable features is its courtyard garden, which is filled with citrus trees, floral plants, and fountains. It's ideal for getting away from the heat and having some peaceful time. The palace also provides breathtaking views of Seville's roofs, reminding you of the city's rich history.

San Marcos Church

San Marcos Church is one of those sites that receives far less attention than it deserves, but that's part of its appeal to me. This 14th-century church, located in the Ferian area, is a remarkable example of Mudejar architecture, combining Gothic and Islamic design elements in a unique Andalusian style.

The first time I visited San Marcos, I was captivated by its simple façade, which contrasted with the rich features found within. The church's tower, with its exquisite arches and brickwork, resembles a minaret, a tribute to Seville's Moorish heritage. Inside, the church is a serene sanctuary with lofty vaulted ceilings and stunning stained-glass windows that shed colorful light across the stone floors.

San Marcos' closeness to the local community adds to its unique character. It's more than just a historical landmark; it's an active element of Seville's daily life. On weekends, local families frequently attend mass, and during Semana Santa, the church plays a major role in the city's famed parade.

Seville is a city that slowly unveils itself, and its hidden gems await anyone prepared to venture off the usual road. Whether it's the tranquil Murillo Gardens, the historic city walls, or the aromatic courtyards hidden behind inconspicuous doors, these lesser-known gems provide a window into the city's spirit. So, the next time you're in Seville, make a detour, get lost, and see what hidden jewels you can find. You never know what you will find.

Chapter 12

WHAT NOT TO DO IN SEVILLE

Seville is a wonderful city filled with vivid culture, history, and culinary pleasures. It's easy to fall in love with the city's charm, but as with any place, there are some unwritten regulations and local customs. As someone who has made a few mistakes along the way (I'm still healing from the time I unintentionally strolled into a local festival wearing gym shorts), I've learned that there are several things you should avoid doing in Seville. So, here's my guide to what not to do, based on personal experience, humor, and the occasional lesson learned the hard way!

Avoiding Tourist Traps

Seville is a popular tourist destination, and with good reason: it is full of breathtaking landmarks, gorgeous architecture, and a rich history. However, where there are tourists, there are tourist traps, and if you're not vigilant, you might easily end up overpaying for a mediocre experience.

One of the most prevalent traps is restaurants near prominent landmarks such as the Cathedral or the Alcázar. While it's tempting to take a seat on a terrace with a perfect view of the Giralda, avoid the desire unless you're willing to pay a fortune for poor meals. Instead, take a short stroll away from the big squares to uncover more authentic restaurants with better rates and food. My advice? Visit the Triananeighborhood or Santa Cruz's small alleyways, where locals eat and where you can get food that hasn't been adapted to tourist tastes.

Another popular tourist trap is horse-drawn carriages. They are beautiful, yes, but they also come with exorbitant costs and questionable ethics. If you're dead bent on riding in one, make sure to haggle the fee up front. However, Seville is best explored on foot, where you can discover hidden gems that are not marked on any map.

Tip Etiquette in Seville

If you're from the United States or another tipping-heavy society, you may feel compelled to offer a generous tip after a meal in Seville. But wait—tipping in Spain, particularly in Seville, is a very different ballgame. Tipping is much more subdued here, and no one will give you the side eye if you leave without tipping, especially in casual settings.

A basic rule of thumb is to round up the bill to the closest euro or leave a modest amount of change if the service was exceptional. In more premium places, a 5% tip is considered generous. Leaving 20% will most likely result in a bewildered face and a "gracias," but it is not required. I discovered this after leaving a particularly substantial tip, which prompted a server to chase me down the street, arguing I had given too much. Lesson learned!

Don't tip in bars unless you're feeling especially festive. When ordering a caña (small beer) or vino tinto in a tapas bar, merely paying the bill is acceptable. Save your euros for another round of croqueta!

Dress Codes for Religious Sites

Seville is home to some of Europe's most spectacular ecclesiastical sites, such as the Seville Cathedral and the Basilica de la Macarena. While these places are open to tourists, they are still active houses of worship, so dress accordingly if you do not want to be respectfully asked to leave.

I'll admit that I once made the rookie mistake of arriving at the cathedral on a hot summer day wearing a sleeveless dress. I was greeted with a harsh look and a compassionate nun who handed me a shawl at the door—bare shoulders were not going to make it in this holy place.

When visiting religious sites in Seville, dress modestly. This means no bare shoulders, shorts, or very showing attire. A decent rule of thumb is to keep your legs and shoulders covered. If you're going during the summer and risk melting in the Andalusian sun (which is a genuine possibility), bring a lightweight scarf to drape over your shoulders when you enter a church or cathedral.

Overpacking For A Day Trip

When I first started taking day trips from Seville, I prepared as if I were going on a month-long expedition: various layers, food, two bottles of water, a guidebook, sunscreen, sunglasses, a cap, and (just in case) an umbrella. After dragging what felt like half of my apartment on a vacation to Córdoba, I immediately realized that less is more.

Day trips in Andalusia can involve a lot of walking, especially if you visit cities like Ronda or Carmona, which have steep hills and narrow alleys. Overpacking will leave you sweating and sore at the end of the day (and probably resent your luggage selection). Instead, pack lightly. A little bag containing a bottle of water, sunscreen, and perhaps a light jacket for the evening is generally plenty. If you're worried about getting hungry, make a pit stop at a café or market along the way—eating impromptu snacks is half the fun of traveling in Spain, after all.

Conversely, underpacking might be a mistake. For a day trip to Doñana National Park or other rural locations, pack appropriate walking shoes and a sun hat. Believe me, hiking through a natural reserve in flip-flops is not as glamorous as it sounds.

Dining Hours: When Locals Eat

When I first arrived in Seville, one of the most noticeable cultural differences was the dining schedule. Coming from a country where lunch is served at noon and dinner at 6 p.m., I quickly discovered that eating at these times in Spain is like walking into a ghost town. Meals in Seville are slow affairs, and you'll need to adapt to the local rhythm if you don't want to end up sitting in an empty restaurant, staring wistfully at a closed kitchen.

Lunch, the largest meal of the day in Seville, is normally served about 2 p.m. And 4 p.m. It's a lengthy, languid meal, often followed by a siesta, so don't anticipate any post-lunch activities to begin until later in the afternoon. When I initially arrived, I made the mistake of turning up for lunch around noon, only to find the restaurant entirely vacant and the staff giving me a look like, "You poor, clueless foreigner."

Dinner is even later. Most locals don't eat dinner until 9 or 10 p.m., and in the summer, folks can dine as late as 11 p.m. My first week in Seville, I remember going down to supper at 7:30 p.m., feeling happy that I'd "stayed up late" for dinner—only to discover that the restaurant wouldn't open for another hour.

The good news is that tapas bars have a slightly more flexible schedule, so if you're looking for a bite between regular meal hours, you'll generally find a bar serving jamón ibérico and a glass of tinto de verano. However, if you want to enjoy Seville like a local, set your internal clock and embrace late dining hours. Bonus: less crowds and greater people-watching.

Street Scams to Look Out For

While Seville is generally a secure city, like with any popular tourist destination, there are a few street scams to be wary of. The good news is that they are usually quite straightforward to avoid if you know what to look for.

One of the most prevalent scams is offering "free" rosemary sprigs. Women in the tourist-heavy regions around the Cathedral and the Alcázar frequently offer little sprigs of rosemary, claiming they are a gift. If you accept it, they will demand payment—sometimes angrily. My advice? Simply keep walking and say a polite but firm "No, gracias." It's not worth the trouble, and rosemary is far more pleasurable when used in cooking than as part of a street scam.

Another scam to watch out for is the "tricky waiter" act. While this does not occur frequently, I have heard of a few travelers who have been overcharged for meals, particularly in the more touristic areas of town. Always double-check your bill to ensure you have not been charged for products you did not order. If something seems wrong, don't be hesitant to ask for explanation.

Finally, keep an eye out for pickpockets, particularly in crowded areas such as markets or during festivals. Seville's pickpockets are expert at their trade, but you may simply avoid being a victim by keeping your belongings safe. I always carry a crossbody bag that zips closed and keeps it in front of me, especially in congested locations.

Seville is an easy city to fall in love with, but like with any location, there are a few things to avoid if you want to have the best trip possible. Whether it's avoiding tourist traps, adjusting to the local dining schedule, or being conscious of clothing requirements at religious sites, a little insider information may go a long way toward making your stay in Seville enjoyable and stress-free. So pack light, eat late, and most importantly—enjoy the charm that this city has to offer!

Chapter 13

UNIQUE SHOPPING EXPERIENCES

Shopping in Seville has an undoubtedly unique appeal. It's more than just buying a memento to take home; it's about immersing yourself in the city's rich cultural heritage, craftsmanship, and traditions. As someone who has spent many days wandering Seville's stores, marketplaces, and boutiques, I can assure you that shopping here is more than just a transaction; it is an experience. Whether you're looking for the ideal ceramic tile from Triana or a handcrafted flamenco dress, Seville has a way of making even the tiniest purchases feel like you're bringing a piece of the city's soul home. So, let me take you on a tour of some of Seville's most unusual shopping experiences, where each item has a story.

Local Handicrafts and Artisanal Goods

Seville is a city that values tradition, and the many local handicrafts reflect this. Whether you're in the heart of the city or exploring the more tucked-away areas, you'll come across shops selling artisanal goods that represent the region's history and craftsmanship. One of the things I've always liked about shopping in Seville is that each item feels unique—whether it's a handwoven shawl, a leather bag, or a piece of wrought-iron decor, the craftspeople here take care in their craft.

La Recova, a modest, adorable shop in the Alameda de Hércules district, is one of my favorite places to browse for handcrafted items. This tiny jewel specializes on traditional Andalusian items, such as brightly colored mantones de Manila (embroidered silk shawls) and esparto grass baskets that are both sturdy and elegant. I purchased a hand-painted ceramic jug from here, and every time I pour water from it at home, I am transported to the sunny streets of Seville.

Artífices, a collective of local craftsmen, sells a variety of distinctive items, including pottery, leather goods, jewelry, and woodwork. This shop, located near the Cathedral, provides a little bit of everything and is ideal for finding a uniquely Sevillian gift (for yourself or others). The artists are frequently present in the shop and are always eager to discuss their work, adding a personal touch to your purchase.

Ceramics from Triana

If you want to buy pottery in Seville, you must travel to Triana. This district, located across the river from the city center, is at the heart of Seville's pottery culture. For generations, Triana artists have created the azulejos (tiles) and pottery that adorn so many of Seville's buildings, and wandering through the area, you can still witness the impact of this rich past.

One of the first things you'll notice about Triana is the number of ceramic stores. Every window is adorned with exquisitely painted tiles, plates, and vases, each one a work of beauty. Cerámica Santa Ana, a family-owned pottery factory that has been in operation for almost a century, is one of my favorite shops. going into their workshop seems like going back in time— the walls are packed with shelves filled with hand-painted tiles, and you can even watch the artists at work, delicately painting each piece by hand.

If you want something truly unique, try requesting a custom piece. Many of Triana's ceramic businesses provide this option, allowing you to design a one-of-a-kind souvenir that matches your individual flair. I previously had a set of ceramic house numbers produced for my front door, and whenever I return home, I am reminded of Seville's brilliant colors and artistic energy.

Of course, if you don't want to take home a full set of tiles (believe me, they can be heavy), there are lots of smaller ceramic pieces that make great gifts or mementos. I can't tell you how many ceramic coasters and small tiles I've taken back for friends—they're easy to transport and offer a touch of Seville to any home.

Flamenco Fashion: Where To Buy

Flamenco is not merely a dance; it is a way of life in Seville. And if you visit during the Feria de Abrilor or any local event, you'll see that everyone is dressed in wonderful, vivid flamenco dresses. The traje de flamenca, with its ruffles, brilliant colors, and polka dots, is an iconic symbol of Andalusian culture, and even if you don't intend to dance, shopping for flamenco attire is an unforgettable experience.

Calle Cuna, a boulevard in the city center lined with businesses specializing in traditional Andalusian fashion, is one of the greatest places to shop for flamenco outfits and accessories. El Duende and Carmen Acedo sell a wide range of flamenco trajes, from traditional polka-dotted patterns to more modern renditions. Even if you don't want to buy a whole flamenco dress, these businesses sell accessories such as peinetas (decorative combs), mantillas (lace shawls), and flamenco shoes, which make great keepsakes.

One thing I enjoy about shopping for flamenco apparel in Seville is the attention to detail. The dresses are carefully crafted, typically cut to fit perfectly, and the fabric selection is stunning—bright reds, deep blues, and delicate florals. I purchased a modest flamenco shawl during one of my travels, and while I don't use it to dance the sevillanas, it adds a burst of color to my clothing back home.

Flamenco outfits can be found everywhere during the Feria de Abril, but flamenco fashion is also alive and thriving in Seville's boutiques year-round. And who knows. You might just get caught up in the city's enthusiasm and leave with your own ruffled frock.

Shopping at Calle Sierpes

No shopping trip to Seville is complete without a stroll down Calle Sierpes, one of the city's most famous retail alleys. This pedestrianized street goes through the heart of the old town and is dotted with a variety of shops, from traditional to modern. If you want a more traditional shopping experience, Calle Sierpes is the place to go.

As you go down Calle Sierpes, you'll see a little bit of everything: leather items, shoes, apparel, and jewelry. Sombrerería Maquedano, a classic hat business dating back to the 19th century, is a personal favorite on this street. The shop is known for its classic Andalusian sombreros (hats), and I couldn't resist purchasing one for myself. It's a classic wide-brimmed hat, ideal for keeping the sun out during Seville's sweltering summers—and, let's be honest, it gives a unique touch to any ensemble.

If you're looking for shoes, Seville is well-known for its handcrafted leather footwear, and Calle Sierpes contains several shops that specialize in high-quality, locally created shoes. Calzados Sánchez is one of the greatest places to find them, as the shoes are still handmade using traditional methods. The craftsmanship is flawless, and nothing beats the feel of a pair of custom-fitted leather shoes.

Visit Confitería La Campana, one of Seville's oldest pastry shops, to learn about its history. Even if you're not looking for sweets (and who wouldn't be?), the shop's lovely facade and old-world charm are worth a look. While you're there, indulge in a tarta de yema or a polvorón—you won't regret it.

Vintage Finds & Antique Markets

If you enjoy all things vintage, Seville has lots to offer. From antique furniture to vintage apparel, the city is a treasure trove for those who like the thrill of the hunt. One of my favorite spots to look for hidden treasures is the El Jueves Market, a flea market that takes place every Thursday on Calle Feria. This market has existed for centuries and is the place to go if you're seeking for vintage discoveries, antiques, or unusual secondhand products.

The first time I went to El Jueves, I had no idea what to anticipate. However, as I went among the shops, I quickly discovered that this market is a treasure trove of unique and interesting products. You'll discover anything from vintage flamenco costumes to ancient vinyl recordings, antique furniture, and even religious art. I once came across a gorgeous hand-painted ceramic bowl that appeared to have been sitting in someone's attic for decades; it now has a place of pride on my dinner table.

Antigüedades El Patio, an antique boutique tucked away in the Alfalfaneighborhood, is another excellent option for vintage enthusiasts. This business is full with treasures, ranging from old furniture and artwork to vintage lamps and mirrors. The proprietor, a cheerful man with a love of history, is usually eager to tell you the tale behind each piece, and I've spent many afternoons wandering the shop, picturing the lives these artifacts once had.

For vintage apparel, Ropero Vintage is a must-see. Located near Alameda de

Hércules sells antique apparel from the 1950s to the 1980s. Ropero Vintage has something for everyone, whether they want a retro flamenco dress or bell-bottom trousers. I once found a magnificent 1960s cocktail dress here that looked straight out of a movie, and it's still one of my favorite things in my closet.

Seville is a shopper's dream, but it's more than simply the act of shopping; it's about the experience, the tales behind each item, and the connection you feel to the city's rich cultural legacy. Seville has a unique shopping experience, whether you're looking for hand-painted ceramics, trying on a flamenco attire, or browsing the stalls at a flea market. So gather your money (and perhaps an extra luggage), and prepare

to experience the unique riches that this dynamic city
has to offer.

Chapter 14

SEVILLE FOR FAMILIES

Seville, with its brilliant plazas, sun-dappled parks, and rich history, is more than just a playground for adults looking for flamenco thrills and tapas delicacies; it's also a family paradise. While Seville is well-known for its architectural marvels and dramatic festivals, there is also a side of the city geared to keeping younger visitors interested, curious, and happy. Whether you're coming with babies or teenagers, the city has a fascinating blend of attractions suitable for all ages. After spending time visiting Seville with friends and their children, I can attest to the city's family-friendly nature. Let's explore the kid-friendly areas of Seville!

Kid-Friendly Attractions

One of the first places families should visit is Isla Mágica, Seville's own theme park on the Isla de la Cartuja. Trust me when I say Isla Mágica will transport you to a realm of pirates and conquistadors. The park has rides for all ages, including the soothing Círculo del Lago boat ride for toddlers and the thrilling Jaguarroller coaster for older children and adults. And in the summer, the water park area, Agua Mágica, is a lifesaver—because, let's be honest, Seville in July is hot, and this waterpark is the ultimate chill.

The Acuario de Sevilla, or Seville Aquarium, is another excellent family destination, located on the banks of the Guadalquivir River. It's a modest size, making it ideal for families with little children who may lack the strength to spend the entire day exploring. You'll see a variety of aquatic life, including colorful fish, sea turtles, jellyfish, and sharks. The shark tunnel is particularly popular with children (and some slightly timid adults). I'll never forget seeing one of my friend's kids stand wide-eyed as a shark glided overhead, confident it was going to make eye contact!

La Casa de la Ciencia is another excellent option for combining nature and history. This science museum, located in a lovely old structure, features interactive exhibits on astronomy, biodiversity, and geology. It's created with younger people in mind, so it's not your standard museum experience where you have to speak quietly. Here, children are encouraged to touch, explore, and discover. The planetarium, in particular, is a big hit—whether your child is already a space fan or not, they'll leave ready to conquer the universe.

Parks and Playgrounds in the City

One of Seville's best offerings to families is its abundance of green spaces. With vast open plazas and shady parks, there are plenty of areas for kids to run around and burn off their energy. I've spent many afternoons enjoying Seville's parks, and I can tell you that they're ideal for parents wishing to unwind while their children play.

Parque de María Luisa is the crown jewel of Seville's parks. It's the type of location where you might easily spend hours meandering around shaded walks, riding bikes, or hiring a rowboat on one of the ponds. Don't miss the adjoining Plaza de España, where you may rent a small boat to row around the moat. Even if rowing a boat sounds like something children would like, let's just say the adults had a little more fun figuring out the mechanics!

If your kids need some more action, take them to Parque del Alamillo. This vast park provides ample area for children to explore freely, and the playground is popular with both locals and visitors. Swings, slides, and climbing structures are available for children to explore as you rest and enjoy the peaceful ambiance. The park also includes picnic spots, so you can bring some snacks and have an impromptu picnic—just keep a look out for the many friendly ducks that roam the park.

Another hidden gem is the Murillo Gardens, which are located behind the Alcázar. Although smaller than María Luisa, it's ideal for families seeking a peaceful place to unwind after a day of sightseeing. The grounds are immaculately kept, with plenty of benches for resting, and there's frequently a breeze blowing through the trees, providing much-needed reprieve from the Andalusian sun.

Family-Friendly Restaurants

Dining out with children in Seville is not only convenient, but also enjoyable. The Spaniards adore children, and dining with your children in Seville will never feel awkward. Most restaurants and tapas bars are family-friendly, with child-sized portions or dishes that can be shared. Furthermore, the environment at Seville's restaurants is lively enough that no one will notice if your children become a little noisy.

Los Coloniales, a lively tapas bar with ample quantities and a diverse menu, is one of my favorite places for family lunches. Their croquetas (fried, creamy croquettes filled with ham or chicken) are always popular with children, and the quantity sizes ensure no one goes hungry. Furthermore, the central position in Plaza Cristo de Burgos makes it an ideal stop after a morning of sightseeing.

Bar Alfalfa offers a more informal atmosphere. It's a quiet, laid-back location in the middle of the city, ideal for a family lunch. The staff is really courteous, and the menu includes a good mix of traditional tapas and more contemporary selections. I recommend the tosta de solomillo con queso de cabra (pork loin with goat cheese on toast); it's not especially kid-friendly, but you can sneak a taste in between serving patatas bravasto to the kids.

If your family prefers more international cuisine, Veganista in the Setas de Sevilla is a stylish yet calm alternative that caters to both plant-based and non-vegetarian diners. They provide kid-friendly options like as veggie burgers, fries, and tasty smoothies, making this a great choice for families looking for a departure from typical Spanish cuisine.

Outdoor Adventures: Bike Tours and River Activities

Seville's flat topography and ample bike routes make it an ideal destination for a family cycling tour. Renting a bike and touring the city on two wheels is not only enjoyable, but it is also an excellent method to cover a lot of ground without tiring little feet. There are many of bike rental shops throughout the city, and many of them offer child-sized bikes or bike seats for smaller children.

The trail along the Guadalquivir River is ideal for families. It's a safe, picturesque path with beautiful views of the river, and you can stop along the way to explore landmarks like the Torre del Oroor or relax at one of the riverbank cafes. If your children are feeling brave, consider hiring a quadricycle—four-person motorcycles that resemble miniature vehicles. They are ideal for families, and the kids will enjoy pretending to drive!

For water-loving families, there is no better way to discover Seville than by taking a riverboat cruise. The Guadalquivir River runs through the heart of the city, providing a unique viewpoint on Seville's prominent structures. You can take a number of boat tours, ranging from short 30-minute journeys to longer cruises with commentary on the city's history. My favorite method to explore the river is to rent a paddleboat—there's something immensely enjoyable about going along the river with the kids pretending to be pirates looking for treasure.

Educational Museums for Children

Seville has full of wonderful museums, although some are more family-friendly than others. If you're traveling with young children, you'll be pleased to hear that the city boasts numerous museums that cater to curious minds with interactive exhibits and hands-on learning opportunities.

The Casa de la Ciencia, also known as the House of Science, is a popular family museum. Located in the historic Peru Pavilion from the 1929 Ibero-American

Expo, this museum provides a pleasant and interesting introduction to the natural world. The exhibits cover everything from dinosaurs and insects to space exploration and climate change, and many of the displays are interactive, allowing children to participate in the learning process. The planetarium is a standout feature, with daily programs that take children on a trip through the cosmos.

Another excellent museum for children is the Museo del Baile Flamenco, which was founded by the great flamenco dancer Cristina Hoyos. While flamenco may not seem like a kid-friendly activity, this museum does a fantastic job of teaching children to the art form in a pleasant and approachable way. The interactive exhibits allow children to practice clapping flamenco rhythms and even dress up in traditional flamenco clothes. If your family is lucky enough to see one of the live flamenco performances, you'll be astounded by the dancers' energy and passion—it's an experience that will instill a new appreciation for this classic Spanish art form.

For history buffs, the Archivo de Indias is another excellent choice. While the documents themselves may not be particularly exciting for younger children, the museum does include some fascinating displays on Spain's exploration of the New World, including maps, ship models, and relics that will pique the interest of interested children. The building, a UNESCO World Heritage monument, is worth seeing for its beautiful architecture alone.

Seville is an excellent family destination, offering a unique blend of culture, history, and outdoor adventure that will keep both children and adults entertained. Seville is a welcoming city for families, offering activities such as rowing boats in Parque de María Luisa, seeing the science museum, and enjoying kid-approved tapas. So pack the stroller, bring lots of sunscreen, and prepare for a memorable family outing. Just don't be surprised if the youngsters want to come back next year!

Chapter 15

SEVILLE FOR COUPLES

Seville has an undeniable magical quality, and for couples, it feels tailor-made for romance. From the winding, cobblestone alleyways of the Barrio Santa Cruz to the calm, secret courtyards where time appears to slow down, Seville exudes beauty and intimacy at every step. I've spent many hours strolling through the city's most romantic corners, and each time I fall further in love with both the place and the people I'm with. Whether you're celebrating a honeymoon, an anniversary, or simply seeking an escape from the hustle and bustle of everyday life, Seville is the ideal setting for a love tale. Let's look at some of the most romantic moments you may have in this wonderful city.

Romantic Rooftop Dinners

Nothing says romance like a candlelit supper with stunning views, and Seville has plenty of amazing rooftop venues to sweep you and your sweetheart off your feet. One of my favorite settings for a romantic dinner is La Terraza del EME at the EME Catedral Hotel. Perched just across from the famed Giralda, this rooftop patio provides incomparable views of Seville's cathedral, its spires shining softly in the evening light as the city below twinkles.

There's something very magical about sitting here with a glass of Cavain and watching the sunset paint the sky in pink and orange. The menu focuses on modern Spanish cuisine, with fresh, seasonal ingredients and artistically presented meals. I recommend the sea bass—it's delicate, tasty, and goes well with the lovely surroundings. The setting is small but not overtly formal, making it an excellent place to linger over dessert while the city comes to life below.

For a more unique experience, visit El Pasaje, a tiny rooftop restaurant located in Santa Cruz's labyrinth. It does not offer the broad vistas of some of the larger roofs, but what it lacks in size it more than makes up for in character. With fairy lights draped across the patio and a faint hum of flamenco in the background, it feels like a secret garden floating above Seville's roofs. Order a bottle of local wine, have some tapas, and enjoy the warmth of a Spanish evening.

Horse-Drawn Carriage Rides Through the City

Yes, I understand that horse-drawn carriage rides can seem like the ideal tourist activity. But believe me, in Seville, they are something else entirely. There's something immensely beautiful about being gently carried through the city's narrow streets, the sound of the horse's hooves echoing down the cobblestone lanes as you pass past antique houses, orange trees, and softly shimmering street lamps.

The carriages, known as coches de caballos, can be seen waiting in Plaza del Triunfón near the cathedral, and many of the drivers provide guided tours. You can choose between a brisk 30-minute ride and an hour or more, depending on how immersed you are in the moment. I recommend taking the longer route through Parque de María Luisa and Plaza de España, two of the city's most charming sites.

The carriage ride's slower speed allows you to notice features of Seville that you may miss when walking— tiny balconies loaded with flowers, hidden courtyards peeking out from behind wrought-iron gates, and the faint murmur of Sevillanos going about their evening routines. It's a peaceful, nostalgic way to see the city, and doing it with someone you care about makes it even more magical.

Scenic Boat Rides on the Guadalquivir

Few things are more romantic than drifting slowly down a river with your spouse by your side, and Seville's Guadalquivir River provides the ideal setting for a picturesque boat trip. The river, which runs through the city, provides breathtaking views of some of Seville's most recognizable buildings, including the Torre del Oroto and the colorful Triana neighborhood. There are numerous options for boat excursions, including guided tours, private rentals, and something a little more hands-on.

For a more traditional experience, take one of the river excursions that depart on a regular basis from the piers near the Torre del Oro. These boats provide a leisurely way to see the sites, with narration provided to provide some context for the monuments you'll pass along the route. But, if you're like me and prefer a little more adventure, you can hire a kayak or paddleboat and cruise the river yourself. There's something magical about being on the water, surrounded by the grandeur of the city and only hearing the river and the occasional seagull overhead.

Consider arranging your boat ride around sunset to provide an unforgettable experience. As the sun sets below the horizon, the sky turns golden and the city's reflection shimmers on the lake. It's the ideal time to steal a kiss and enjoy Seville's breathtaking splendor.

Sunset Walks Around the Alcázar Gardens

The Real Alcázar of Seville is one of the city's most well-known buildings, and for good reason: it's an architectural marvel that combines Moorish, Gothic, Renaissance, and Baroque styles, leaving you dumbfounded. However, for lovers, the true magic of the Alcázar lies in its gardens. The sprawling and tranquil gardens are a haven of peace in the center of the city, complete with blooming flowers, trickling fountains, and shaded pathways that appear to be created for romantic strolls.

One of my favorite times to visit the Alcázar gardens is late afternoon, right before sunset, when the crowds have dispersed and golden light shines through the trees. Walking hand in hand through the gardens, you'll come across peaceful places where you may relax on a bench and take in the beauty of your surroundings. The gardens are packed with orange and lemon trees, whose smell fills the air, while the sound of birdsong serves as the perfect backdrop.

For a romantic moment, visit the Baths of Doña María de Padilla, a complex of underground rainwater tanks with surreal beauty. The chilly, dark room is illuminated by sunlight filtering through a single aperture, and the motionless water provides a mirror-like image that feels fantastic. It's one of those places where you can't help but pause and enjoy the moment.

Hidden Courtyards for Quiet Moments

Seville's courtyards, or patios, are one of the city's most appealing characteristics, and they're ideal for couples looking for a quiet moment away from people. These hidden beauties, tucked behind inconspicuous doorways, are frequently filled with lush flora, flowing fountains, and brilliant azulejos (ceramic tiles). One of the best things about Seville is that you can come into these courtyards simply by chance, turning a corner or peering through an open door to find a secret garden waiting to be discovered.

One of the most gorgeous courtyards I've seen is at the Casa de Pilatos, a stunning palace that blends Gothic, Renaissance, and Mudejar architecture. The main courtyard, with its elaborate tilework and center fountain, is stunning, but the smaller, more private courtyards are the most personal. There's something deeply romantic about sitting on a stone bench, surrounded by the aroma of jasmine and the soothing sound of water, with the city just beyond the gates.

Another hidden courtyard worth hunting out is the Patio de los Naranjos, which is part of the Seville Cathedral complex. This orange-tree-filled courtyard provides a peaceful respite from the hectic streets outside, and it's the ideal location to rest and meditate after touring the cathedral. The aroma of the orange flowers, along with the soft light flowing through the trees, creates a timeless ambience.

Seville has a way of awakening the romantic in everyone. Whether you're having a rooftop supper beneath the stars, taking a sunset stroll through the Alcázar gardens, or sneaking a quiet moment in a secluded courtyard, the city is the ideal setting for love. So, take your partner's hand and discover the beauty of Seville together, making memories that will stay long after you leave this lovely place.

Chapter 16

SEVILLE'S RELIGIOUS HERITAGE

Seville's skyline is lined with soaring bell towers, beautiful domes, and complex stone sculptures that allude to the city's rich religious history. Whether you're a history buff, an architect, or someone looking for a quiet moment of introspection, Seville has a plethora of sacred places that show the city's interesting and complicated spiritual history. I've spent many hours strolling through Seville's churches, monasteries, and convents, and I can assure you that the religious monuments are as much about storytelling as they are about devotion. Each one is a window into the past, revealing glimpses of a city fashioned by centuries of dedication, strife, and creativity.

Let's take a tour of some of Seville's most notable religious landmarks, each with its own distinct story and atmosphere.

Visiting the Seville Cathedral

You can't discuss Seville's religious past without mentioning the Seville Cathedral, the world's largest Gothic cathedral and an architectural marvel that will astound even the most experienced traveler. I recall my first sight of the cathedral: strolling down a narrow street, I turned a corner, and there it was, towering over me like a big stone guardian, its beautiful carvings casting long shadows in the late afternoon sun.

The Catedral de Santa María de la Sede, erected in the 15th century, replaced a prior mosque. In fact, the cathedral's famed bell tower, La Giralda, was previously the mosque's minaret and now serves as a symbol of Seville's distinctive blend of Christian and Moorish design. Climbing to the top of La Giralda is a must-do; there are no stairs, only a series of ramps constructed to allow horseback riders to mount the tower. The views from the summit are simply magnificent, with a 360-degree panoramic of Seville's twisting lanes, orange groves, and distant hills.

The cathedral's sheer size is breathtaking. The high vaulted ceilings appear to approach the heavens, and the light spilling through the stained glass windows casts a warm, unearthly glow over the area. One of the attractions is the Capilla Mayor, or main altar, which has an impressively detailed gold altarpiece showing scenes from Christ's life. It's supposed to be the world's largest altarpiece, and standing in front of it, I couldn't help but admire the workmanship and dedication required to make something so exquisite.

Of course, there is the Tomb of Christopher Columbus—yes, the same Christopher Columbus. His remains (or a portion of them, depending on whose historian you ask) are housed in an elaborate mausoleum borne by four allegorical figures representing the kingdoms of Castile, León, Aragón, and Navarre. Whether or not Columbus is present in Seville, the tomb is an outstanding site that serves as a reminder of the city's importance throughout the Age of Exploration.

The Monastery of San Isidoro del Campo

While the Seville Cathedral receives all of the attention, there are numerous more religious buildings in and around Seville that are equally fascinating—if a little further off the beaten path. One such location is the Monastery of San Isidoro del Campo, which is only a short drive from the city near the hamlet of Santiponce.

Alonso Pérez de Guzmán founded this monastery in 1301; it is a hidden gem for anybody interested in medieval art, history, or architecture. The first time I went, I was struck by the peaceful, even spooky aura of the location. The cloisters, with their modest but exquisite stone arches, appear to have remained unchanged for ages, and going through them feels like stepping back in time.

The true riches of San Isidoro del Campo are hidden inside, where the walls are covered with exquisite paintings and Mudejar carvings that relate stories from both Christian and Islamic traditions. One of the most spectacular elements is the monastery's main altarpiece, a late Gothic masterwork depicting scenes from the life of Saint Isidore, Seville's patron saint. The monastery is particularly well-known for its role in the early Spanish Reformation, as it housed several monks who translated the Bible into Spanish, which did not go down well with the Inquisition.

San Isidoro del Campo lacks the grandeur of the Seville Cathedral, yet it has a peaceful beauty all its own. If you want to get away from the throng and discover a lesser-known aspect of Seville's religious heritage, this monastery is well worth a visit.

La Cartuja: Seville's Charterhouse

For a unique experience, visit the Monastery of Santa María de las Cuevas, also known as La Cartuja. This old Carthusian monastery on La Cartuja Island has a fascinatingly diversified history, having served as a place of prayer, a pottery factory, and the final resting place of Christopher Columbus (yes, again).

La Cartuja is currently part of Seville's Centro Andaluz de Arte Contemporáneo (Andalusian Center for Contemporary Art), making it a perfect marriage of the ancient and modern. The first time I went, I found myself meandering through serene cloisters one minute and admiring cutting-edge art pieces the next. It's a site where centuries of history mix, resulting in a distinct ambiance that is both contemplative and uplifting.

One of the most remarkable characteristics of La Cartuja is its link to Columbus. According to legend, Columbus' remains were carried here after his death by his son, Diego Columbus, and remained in the monastery's chapel for several decades until being transported to Seville Cathedral. While his remains are no longer at La Cartuja, the monastery's history as the final resting place for one of history's most famous explorers adds to the site's allure.

Today, La Cartuja is one of Seville's most distinctive religious venues, with its combination of ancient monastic buildings and contemporary art shows. If you value both history and modern inventiveness, this is a must-see destination.

The Convent of Santa Clara

One of Seville's best-kept secrets is the Convent of Santa Clara, a quiet sanctuary nestled in the city's core. This ancient monastery, founded in the 13th century, is now a cultural institution that retains much of its original splendor. The convent is tucked away in the San Lorenzone area, and although being only a short walk from the city center, it feels like a world apart.

When I first visited Santa Clara, I was struck by the sense of tranquillity that pervades the area. The convent's cloisters are basic yet lovely, with whitewashed walls, arching colonnades, and a central courtyard filled with orange trees. It's the ideal place to rest for a while and enjoy the tranquility of your surroundings, which is frequently difficult to locate in the city's busier areas.

One of the Convent of Santa Clara's main attractions is its chapel, which has an impressive collection of religious art, including numerous works by Zurbarán, one of Spain's most famous Baroque artists. The chapel's altar, with its finely carved wooden retablo, is a work of art in its own right, and the soft light streaming through the stained glass windows contributes to the mood of calm devotion.

What makes Santa Clara even more unique is its status as a cultural hub. The convent frequently holds exhibitions, concerts, and performances, so there is always something going on. It's a place where history, art, and culture coexist harmoniously, making it a must-see for anybody interested in Seville's religious and creative traditions.

Iglesia del Salvador

Last but not least, the Iglesia del Salvador is one of Seville's most significant—and beautiful—churches. Located just a short walk from the cathedral, this baroque jewel is frequently overshadowed by its more famous neighbor, yet it is a treasure in its own right.

The Iglesia del Salvador was erected on the site of a former mosque, and its architecture, like that of the cathedral, bears witness to its Islamic origins. The church's towering exterior is a masterwork of Baroque style, with beautiful carvings and statues attracting your attention higher as you approach. Inside, the church is as spectacular, with soaring ceilings, gilded altars, and ornate chapels.

One of the Iglesia del Salvador's features is the Retablo Mayor, a massive altarpiece that dominates the main chapel. It's an explosion of gold and detail, with scenes from Christ's and other saints' lives. Standing in front of it, I couldn't help but be overwhelmed by the piece's sheer size and craftsmanship—it's one of those moments that reminds you of the power of holy art.

The church also exudes a great sense of camaraderie. During Semana Santa, the Iglesia del Salvador is a focal point in the city's famous processions, and the atmosphere within and outside the church is tangible. If you're fortunate enough to visit during one of these events, you'll get a sense of how closely faith and culture are entwined in Seville.

Seville's religious legacy is as varied and extensive as the city itself. From the grandeur of the cathedral to the peaceful beauty of secret convents and monasteries, each location provides a look into the spiritual core of this enchanted city. Whether you're a religious pilgrim, a history buff, or simply a curious traveler, Seville's sacred locations will undoubtedly leave a lasting impact.

So, take your time, explore with an open heart, and let the city's religious past unfold before you, one gorgeous site at a time.

Chapter 17

SEVILLE'S ART AND ARCHITECTURE

Seville is a city that proudly displays its heritage. Every direction you turn unveils a new masterpiece, whether it's a soaring Gothic cathedral, an intricately tiled Moorish castle, or a modern work of street art that stops you cold. As someone who has spent many days exploring the streets of this dynamic city, I can tell you that Seville's art and architecture are like a living museum, with each style and detail telling a portion of the city's rich and multifaceted history. From the grandeur of the Seville Cathedral to the colorful, rebellious paintings of the Alameda area, Seville has something for every art and architecture enthusiast.

Let's take a deep dive into the various styles and periods that shaped Seville's creative landscape. Trust me when I say that the city's diversity, attractiveness, and occasionally weird humor will astound you.

Gothic Masterpieces and Moorish Influences

Seville's cultural and architectural history dates back to the collision of two worlds: Gothic and Moorish. This is particularly obvious at the Seville Cathedral, the world's largest Gothic cathedral. Walking inside, you're struck by its enormous size: massive stone columns, elaborately carved ceilings, and the warm glow of stained glass filtering the sunshine. My first visit to the cathedral seemed like I had entered a hallowed tunnel, with each echo of footsteps serving as a reminder of the millennia of history buried within its walls.

What is remarkable about Seville's architecture is how it combines Gothic and Moorish features. For example, the cathedral's bell tower, La Giralda, was previously a minaret from a mosque that existed on the same location. The tower's form, with its narrow, beautiful arches and ornamental brickwork, exemplifies the Moorish influence that runs across Seville. Climbing to the top (by ramps, not stairs!) rewards you with panoramic views of the city, and you can practically hear the muezzin's call to prayer resounding from the tower centuries before.

What I like best about Seville's Gothic and Moorish blend is how spontaneous it feels. This isn't a city that's locked in a certain architectural period. Instead, Seville has combined elements from each era and culture to create something entirely its own. As a result, the metropolis feels both ancient and contemporary, a living testament to coexistence and cultural exchange.

The Mudejar Style of Alcázar

While the Seville Cathedral is the city's most well-known Gothic edifice, the Real Alcázar is a spectacular example of Mudejar architecture, which originated on the Iberian Peninsula as a fusion of Christian and Muslim influences. Simply said, visiting the Alcázar feels like entering a fairy tale. The first time I stepped through its beautiful gates, I felt as if I had been transported to another world—a realm of elaborate tilework, lush gardens, and fountains that appear to dance with every trickle of water.

The Mudejar style is distinguished by geometric patterns, bright tiles, and the use of horseshoe arches, which are a trademark of Islamic architecture. In the Alcázar, these components work in perfect harmony. Every room feels like a work of art, from the beautifully detailed tiles that cover the walls to the wooden ceilings that have been carved with such accuracy that you'll find yourself staring up at them for much longer than planned.

The Patio de las Doncellas (Maidens' Courtyard) is one of my favorite sites in the Alcázar. The courtyard is an open-air environment enclosed by magnificent arches and featuring a long reflecting pool in the center. The water's surface reflects the intricate stone sculptures, resulting in a very relaxing sensation of quiet and harmony. It's one of those spots where time seems to slow down and all you want to do is take in the scenery.

The gardens of the Alcázar are equally gorgeous, with orange trees, jasmine, and bougainvillea that appear to blossom all year. Fountains, pavilions, and even a labyrinth await you as you wind your way through the maze of walkways. I once spent a whole afternoon getting lost (literally) in the gardens, only to emerge at twilight with the aroma of orange blossoms still in the air.

Baroque Churches and Palaces

As you continue to explore Seville, you'll note a shift in the city's architecture—away from the geometric perfection of Mudejar and toward the extravagance of the Baroque period. Seville's Baroque churches and palaces are nothing short of spectacular, with elaborate façade, gilded interiors, and delicate stucco work. It's as if the architects thought that "more is more" and went all out with their creations.

The Iglesia del Salvador is one of Seville's most spectacular specimens of Baroque architecture. This church, located just a few blocks from the cathedral, is a work of art with its swirling stucco, gold leaf, and larger-than-life figures. Walking inside, you're confronted with a sensory overload—the rich colors, ornate embellishments, and sheer size of the place. It's nearly too much to process at once, but in the greatest possible way. The first time I stepped inside, I couldn't help but laugh—it felt like I'd stumbled upon the set of an over-the-top opera production.

Another Baroque beauty is the Palacio de San Telmo, a former seminary that now houses the Andalusian government. The palace's exterior is a riot of sculptural elements, with cherubs, saints, and mythological figures all competing for attention. It's one of those structures that nearly begs you to stop and appreciate it, if only to see how many distinct faces are etched into the masonry.

What I admire about Seville's Baroque architecture is that it is not subtle. It is intended to be bold, dramatic, and—let's be honest—a touch ostentatious. And it fits well in with Seville's vibrant atmosphere.

Contemporary Art Galleries in Seville

Seville's past is written in its cathedrals, palaces, and historic alleyways, but the city also has a thriving contemporary art scene. After spending hours (or days) admiring the city's historic art and architecture, it's nice to get into something more modern.

The Centro Andaluz de Arte Contemporáneo (CAAC), housed in the old Monastery of Santa María de las Cuevas on La Cartuja Island, is a top destination for contemporary art in Seville. The contrast between the old monastery and cutting-edge contemporary art is stunning, and it's one of those locations where you feel like you're always being shocked. One moment you're strolling through a centuries-old cloister, and the next you're standing in front of a gigantic, abstract sculpture that appears to defy gravity.

The CAAC features recurring exhibitions by both local and international artists, so there is always something new to view. I also like how the exhibitions frequently address topics of Andalusian identity, history, and politics—so you're looking at modern art while remaining very much grounded in the spirit of Seville.

For a more intimate experience, visit the Galería Rafael Ortizin in the Arenal district. This modest gallery showcases modern Spanish artists and provides a more intimate experience than larger museums. I stumbled into it by chance one afternoon and ended up spending an hour talking with the gallery owner about Seville's changing art scene. It's one of those hidden jewels that make visiting Seville so enjoyable.

Street Art in Alameda District

Seville may be steeped in history, but it is also a city that celebrates the new, bold, and unconventional—nowhere is this more evident than in the Alameda de Hércules area, Seville's bohemian core and a hotspot for street art.

The Alameda, previously a neglected region, has recently been converted into a busy neighborhood full with bars, cafes, and art venues. It's the kind of area where you may spend hours exploring the colorful murals, graffiti, and street installations around every turn. The walls of the Alameda tell stories—some political, some personal, but always with a sense of invention and revolt.

One of my favorite paintings in the region is a large, vivid image of Lola Flores, the famous Spanish flamenco dancer and singer. The mural's bold lines and brilliant colors evoke a celebration of Seville's creative legacy, but with a contemporary touch. That's what makes Seville's street art so unique: it bridges the gap between the city's historic past and its current present.

If you want to learn more about Seville's street art community, consider attending one of the guided street art excursions offered in the Alameda. The guides are frequently artists themselves, and they offer intriguing insights into paintings that you might otherwise stroll right by. Furthermore, it's a terrific opportunity to support the local art scene while obtaining a new view on the city.

Seville's art and architecture are as diverse and vibrant as the city itself. Whether you're admiring the

Gothic grandeur of the cathedral, getting lost in the Mudejar splendor of the Alcázar, or taking images of street art on the Alameda, Seville is a city where history and creativity collide in spectacular ways. So take your time, gaze up and about, and let

The city's artistic energy can inspire you—it surely did for me!

Chapter 18

BEST PLACES FOR PHOTOGRAPHY IN SEVILLE

Seville is the type of city that makes you want to bring your camera everywhere, ready to catch those fleeting moments when the light hits just right, the colors explode, and the city's history unfolds in a single shot. As someone who enjoys both exploring and photography, I can assure you that Seville is an absolute dream for anyone trying to capture breathtaking images. From the grandeur of its prominent landmarks to the peaceful beauty of its hidden corners, Seville provides an abundance of photographic opportunity for both amateurs and professionals. Furthermore, with its golden sunsets and lively streets, it's nearly difficult to capture a negative picture here. Almost.

Let's look at some of the top places in Seville to shoot that ideal photos. Whether you're interested in architecture, street scenes, or landscapes, these destinations will provide you with plenty of inspiration—and a couple may surprise you.

The Giralda Tower at Sunset

If you want to capture Seville's skyline in all its beauty, the Giralda Tower is the best location to start. This historic bell tower, which was previously the minaret for the city's mosque, provides some of the most breathtaking views of Seville. But the real magic occurs around sunset. Trust me—climbing those ramps (there are no stairs, just a series of slanted slopes) may leave you breathless, but seeing the sun set over the city is worth every step.

The golden light of sunset casts a pleasant glow over the city, making the Seville Cathedral, rooftops, and even the narrow streets below glisten. I propose timing your climb so that you reach the summit just as the sun begins to set behind the horizon. The play of light and shadow across the city is captivating, and if you're lucky, you might even hear the Giralda's bells sound as the day fades to night. Make sure you bring a wide-angle lens to catch the entire panoramic view!

What I love most about photographing from the Giralda is how the entire city appears to be sprawled out in front of you. The streets appear to wind in all directions, and you can view some of Seville's most famous landmarks from this vantage point. Furthermore, if you time it correctly, you'll get a fantastic photo of the cathedral's spires lighted by the last rays of sunlight.

Colorful Streets of Triana

Across the Guadalquivir River, Triana feels like its own tiny planet. Triana, known for its bright ceramics, flamenco tradition, and lively environment, is one of my favorite spots to explore with my camera. The small alleyways are a riot of color, with vibrantly painted buildings, beautiful tilework, and balconies adorned with flower pots that beg to be photographed.

One of the best things about Triana is that it feels more local and lived-in than some of Seville's more touristy areas. Residents are frequently seen going about their regular routines, such as hanging clothes on their balconies, conversing with neighbors, or riding scooters through the streets. It's an excellent location for street photography, capturing the genuine moments that make a city feel truly alive.

For a classic Triana shot, walk to Calle Betis, the riverside street. From here, you'll have a stunning view of Seville's skyline, with the Torre del Oro and the Giralda in the distance, all reflected in the tranquil waters of the river. Early in the morning or late in the afternoon, the light is ideal for capturing the city's reflection.

Reflective Pools at the Alcázar

The Real Alcázar of Seville is a photographer's dream, with its combination of Mudejar architecture, rich gardens, and beautiful tilework. The reflected lakes in the palace's courtyards, however, are a standout for photography. There's something really lovely about seeing the Alcázar's graceful arches and elaborate carvings reflected perfectly in the motionless lake below.

The Patio de las Doncellas (Courtyard of the Maidens) is one of the ideal places for this. The huge, rectangular pool in the center of the courtyard perfectly reflects the arches and finely tiled walls. If possible, try to visit early in the morning when the crowds are smaller and the light is gentler. The way the early morning light touches the lake, generating delicate ripples, lends a sense of tranquility and serenity to your photographs.

The Baths of Doña María de Padilla, an underground reservoir, are an excellent location for reflection photos. The low lighting and quiet of the river create a hauntingly lovely ambiance, while the arches mirrored in the water provide for some incredibly stunning shots. It can be difficult to capture low light, so bring a tripod if you want to explore with long exposures.

Plaza de España at Dawn

Plaza de España is a well-known monument in Seville and has been photographed extensively. The broad semi-circular plaza, with its elaborate tilework, majestic towers, and gorgeous waterway in the center, is a photographer's dream. For a truly magical experience, visit Plaza de España at dawn.

I understand that getting up early on vacation can feel like a nuisance, but trust me on this. The plaza is nearly deserted in the early morning hours, and the gentle, golden light of the rising sun casts a warm glow around the area. The canal reflections are perfect, the shadows are lengthy and dramatic, and the entire scene appears almost otherworldly without the normal swarms of people. Plus, you'll have the venue mostly to yourself, allowing you to take your time putting up photographs and experimenting with different perspectives.

The central fountain is an excellent focal point for photographs, and the plaza's sweeping curves provide attractive leading lines that bring the viewer's attention to the shot. Take a close look at the azulejos (ceramic tiles) that line the bridges and walls; each one has a story, and the brilliant colors stand out in the early morning light.

Hidden alleyways of Santa Cruz

The Barrio Santa Cruz is Seville's old Jewish enclave, a maze of small, winding lanes that appear to hide a mystery around every corner. This neighborhood is ideal for photographers who enjoy capturing the quieter, more intimate side of Seville. The lanes are lined with whitewashed buildings, colorful shutters, and potted plants spilling over balconies—ideal for those "lost in time" photos that make you feel as if you've walked into another era.

What I enjoy most about photographing in Santa Cruz is the interplay of light and shadow. The streets are so tiny that sunlight only passes through in parts, generating dramatic contrasts that can transform even the most basic entryway or window frame into a work of art. If you're lucky, you may come across a hidden courtyard or catch a glimpse of a tiled fountain through an open gate.

Callejón del Agua, a short lane along the old city walls, is one of Santa Cruz's most photogenic places. The walls are covered with ivy, and the soothing sound of water trickling from hidden fountains enhances the scene. It's a beautiful, tranquil environment where you may spend hours photographing the small things that make Seville so unique.

Scenic Views from the Metropol Parasol

For an entirely different perspective on Seville, visit the Metropol Parasol, a gigantic wooden structure in the city center known affectionately as "Las Setas" (The Mushrooms). The parasol provides one of

Seville's best panoramic vistas, and its sleek, futuristic design stands out against the city's traditional architecture.

The greatest time to photograph the Metropol Parasol is late afternoon or early evening, when the light is soft and the shadows are long. The structure's wooden beams form intriguing geometric patterns, and the view from the top is breathtaking. The entire city is visible from here, including the Giralda, Torre del Oro, and the roofs of Seville's old town.

The parasol itself makes for some excellent architectural images, particularly if you enjoy abstract photography. The structure's flowing lines and organic shapes make it a wonderful challenge to photograph, and the way the light interacts with the wood creates some fascinating textures and shadows.

Seville is a photographer's dream, with its ancient grandeur, active street life, and breathtaking natural light. Whether you're photographing the golden hues of the sunset from the Giralda or getting lost in Triana's colorful streets, the city provides limitless opportunity to produce gorgeous, memorable photographs. So grab your camera, explore with an open heart, and allow Seville's beauty to inspire you. Just remember to put the camera down every now and then to simply enjoy the moment—because sometimes the best memories are those that can't be captured on film.

Chapter 19

SEVILLE'S PARKS AND OUTDOOR SPACES

Seville is well-known for its historical structures, colorful streets, and contagious energy, but it's the parks and outdoor areas that truly elevate the city. These lush oases are more than just a break from the Andalusian sun; they are where Seville's soul emerges to play. Whether you wish to relax in a shaded garden, enjoy a riverfront promenade, or simply relax with a bocadillo on a park seat, Seville's parks are places where life slows down and you can take in the city's rich history and beauty.

Over the course of my stay here, I've realized that Seville's outdoor spaces are much more than just places to rest your feet. They're areas where locals congregate—families with children running wild, couples having romantic picnics, and old friends sharing stories under the shade of orange trees. The city's parks are an important aspect of the local culture, and spending time in them is like witnessing a taste of regular Sevillian life. So, grab your hat, sunscreen, and perhaps a bottle of Tinto de Verano, because we're going to discover some of Seville's most lovely outdoor places.

Parque de María Luisa: A Lush Oasis

Begin with Parque de María Luisa, one of Seville's most iconic green spots. This park, spanning approximately 100 acres, is an absolute haven for anyone who enjoys lush gardens, towering palm trees, and the sound of water trickling from exquisite fountains. My first visit to Parque de María Luisa seemed like entering a secret universe. The city hum appeared to slip away, leaving just birdsong and the delicate rustle of leaves in the breeze.

The park was originally part of the private gardens of the Palacio de San Telmo, but it was donated to the city in 1893 by the Duchess of Montpensier, María Luisa Fernanda de Borbón, thus the name. Today, it serves as Seville's green heart and a popular destination for inhabitants to escape the summer heat.

One of my favorite sites in the park is the Plaza de América, which houses the enormous Museo de Artes y Costumbres Populares and the Museo Arqueológico. The plaza is surrounded by lovely azulejos (ceramic tiles), and there's a central pond where you'll often see a swarm of ducks and the occasional ambitious pigeon eyeing your food. Another must-see is the Fountain of Lions, which features beautiful carvings. Sitting on a bench here, surrounded by beautiful vegetation, is the ideal way to relax after a long day of touring.

The Plaza de España, located at the northern end of Parque de María Luisa, is a must-see for visitors. This is the place to photograph, with its semi-circular construction, Venetian-style bridges, and tiled alcoves symbolizing each Spanish province. I propose taking a rowboat ride around the moat for a wonderfully romantic evening. The park itself is ideal for a leisurely stroll, a bike ride, or simply sitting in a shady location to people-watch.

The Gardens of Alcázar

The Real Alcázar is well-known for its palatial halls and complex Mudejar design, but the gardens hold the true charm for me. The gardens of the Alcázar are sprawling, tranquil, and wonderfully groomed, with orange trees, fountains, and twisting pathways that look like they've been pulled directly out of a fairy tale. It's no surprise that these gardens have hosted everything from royal weddings to Game of Thrones filming sites.

What I like best about the gardens is their diversity. The English Garden's formal, geometric shape, with its straight walks and manicured hedges, contrasts with the Mercury Pond's more wild, untamed beauty, where a bronze statue of the Roman god of trade guards the quiet waters. The reflection of the Alcázar's towers in the pond provides an excellent photo opportunity, particularly early in the morning before the tourists arrive.

The Garden of the Poets is an excellent place to find peace and quiet. This section, with its shaded benches and mosaic-tiled fountains, feels like a hidden sanctuary away from the main pathways. I've spent many afternoons here, reading a book or simply listening to the birds chirping in the trees overhead.

The Alcázar gardens also house one of my favorite oddities: the Labyrinth Garden. It's easy to get lost (literally) in this maze of high hedges, but that's part of the appeal. And if you do find your way out, treat yourself to a leisurely stroll around the Orange Tree Courtyard, where the aroma of citrus permeates the air.

Parque del Alamillo: Nature and Relaxation

For those days when you need a true retreat from the city, Parque del Alamillois is the ideal destination. Located on La Cartuja Island, this huge park has a more raw and untamed vibe than the manicured gardens of María Luisa. It's one of Spain's largest urban parks, and its expansive areas make it ideal for families, runners, bikers, and anybody wishing to spend the day outdoors.

I enjoy visiting Parque del Alamillo on weekends, when the park is bustling with families enjoying picnics, children playing soccer, and couples renting bikes to explore the pathways. The Alamillo Bridge, designed by Santiago Calatrava, lends a startling modern accent to the otherwise serene surroundings and is a favorite destination for both joggers and photographers.

Parque del Alamillo stands out for me because of its sheer variety. You'll discover everything from eucalyptus woods to green meadows, lakes, and even a small farm with kid-friendly animals. There's plenty of room to spread a blanket, have a picnic, and watch the world go by. I once spent a whole afternoon lazing by one of the park's lakes, listening to the distant hum of the city yet feeling far removed from any metropolitan tension.

If you're feeling more athletic, the park also offers paddleboat rentals and cycling lanes that run across the neighborhood. It's an excellent place to chill, reconnect with nature, and experience a more relaxed side of Seville.

The Promenade along the Guadalquivir

One of the characteristics that distinguishes Seville is its link to the Guadalquivir River, which may best be experienced by wandering along the Paseo Marqués de Contadero. This riverside promenade provides breathtaking views of Seville's skyline, the Torre del Oro, and the historic bridges spanning the Guadalquivir.

The promenade is surrounded with palm palms and chairs, making it ideal for a relaxing walk or a sunset run. If you're lucky, you might see one of the city's famous rowing teams exercising on the river, with their boats gliding gently across the water. On weekends, the promenade is bustling with street performers, merchants selling churros and ice cream, and families enjoying the fresh air.

One of the promenade's beauties, in my opinion, is the view of the Triana district across the river. Triana's colorful residences and bustling environment make for great shots, especially late afternoon when the light puts a warm warmth over the landscape. If you're looking for a more energetic excursion, rent a bike or a paddleboard to see the river from a fresh angle.

The Guadalquivir embodies the spirit of Seville—it's a site where history, culture, and daily life coexist, much like the river itself. The riverbank promenade is one of the most soothing places in the city, whether you're walking hand in hand with a loved one, reclining on a seat with a nice book, or simply admiring the vista.

Murillo's Historical Gardens

Tucked away near the Alcázar and Barrio Santa Cruz, the Jardines de Murillo provide a calmer, more intimate alternative to Seville's larger parks. These gardens, named for the Sevillian painter Bartolomé Esteban Murillo, are rich in history and provide a tranquil respite from the neighboring busy streets.

The first thing you'll notice about Jardines de Murillo are the shady walks surrounded with towering palm and aromatic orange trees. The gardens are lined with chairs and fountains, making it ideal for a quiet moment of thought or a relaxing picnic. Locals frequently take their siestas here, lying out on a bench under the dappled shade of a palm tree.

One of the gardens' centerpieces is the Christopher Columbus Monument, a remarkable building with a towering column topped by a lion and two ships, alluding to Columbus' exploration journeys. The monument lends grandeur to the otherwise calm landscape while also serving as a reminder of Seville's historical significance.

What I appreciate best about Jardines de Murillo is that it feels like a hidden gem, despite its proximity to some of Seville's most famous sites. It's a place where you can sit quietly and listen to the city's pleasant sounds—the ideal place to unwind before returning to Seville's historic core.

Seville's parks and outdoor spaces are more than just places to rest your feet; they're fundamental to the city's rhythm and character.

. Seville's green spaces, including Parque de María Luisa, gardens of the Alcázar, and riverbank vistas along the Guadalquivir, provide a peaceful contrast to the city's busy streets. So take your time, locate a quiet area, and allow Seville's natural beauty to do its magic. After all, in such a bustling metropolis, sometimes the best thing you can do is relax and take in the scenery.

Chapter 20

UNIQUE ITINERARIES & SAMPLE PLANS

There are many different ways to explore Seville. Whether you're looking for a brief weekend break, cultural immersion, or to see as much of Seville's art as possible, there's an itinerary for you. The appeal of Seville resides in its capacity to accommodate all types of travelers, from history buffs to budget-conscious backpackers. After spending several days exploring the city's cobblestone streets, lush parks, and hidden gems, I've compiled a list of itineraries to help you make the most of your visit.

These plans are intended to give you a taste of Seville's rich history, culture, and charm, regardless of how long or short your visit. And, because no itinerary should be too rigid (you never know when you'll come upon a flamenco show or a tapas cafe you simply must try), feel free to mix and match. Let's look at some unique methods to experience the magic of Seville.

Weekend Getaway

Only have one weekend in Seville? Don't worry, you can still see and enjoy many of the city's top attractions. This schedule is ideal for first-time tourists who want to explore the sights without feeling overwhelmed.

Day 1:

- Begin your journey by seeing Seville Cathedral and climbing La Giralda for breathtaking views of the city.

- After that, meander through the Barrio Santa Cruz's small streets, pausing for lunch at a local tapas bar such as El Pasaje.

- Spend the afternoon exploring the Real Alcázar. The palace and gardens are huge, so take your time exploring the elaborately tiled rooms and lush courtyards.

- Visit Plaza de España at sunset for a stunning photo opportunity and a pleasant rowboat trip along the canal.

- Wrap up the evening with a flamenco concert at Casa de la Memoria, an intimate venue that provides a genuinely authentic flamenco experience.

Day 2:

- Begin your day with a relaxing stroll around Parque de María Luisa.

- Stop by the Torre del Oro for a quick peek at Seville's maritime heritage before embarking on a Guadalquivir Riverboat excursion.

- In the afternoon, visit the Triananeighborhood to see local culture. Wander down Calle Betis, visit Mercado de Triana, then have a coffee at Bar Las Golondrinas.

- Finish your weekend with dinner at Eslava, one of Seville's most popular tapas bars. Make sure to try the slow-cooked pork ribs; they're legendary.

Cultural Immersion

This cultural immersion program is ideal for those who enjoy learning about a city's history and traditions. Seville is a city that exudes history, and you'll leave with a renewed appreciation for its history, art, and traditions.

Day 1:

- Start your cultural tour with the Archivo de Indias, where you'll learn about Spain's role throughout the Age of Exploration.

- Next, visit the Casa de Pilatos, a stunning palace that combines Renaissance and Mudéjar styles.

- After lunch, head to the Museo de Bellas Artes, one of Spain's most renowned art museums, to see masterpieces by Murillo, Zurbarán, and Velázquez.

- In the evening, see a typical flamenco performance at El Arenal, where you may experience the raw emotion of the dance and music.

Day 2:

- Take a day excursion to Carmona, a medieval village located about 30 minutes from Seville. Explore the Roman necropolis and walk around its small lanes and picturesque squares.

- Return to Seville and see the Hospital de los Venerables, a baroque building that holds a small art collection and provides insight into the city's religious and cultural legacy.

- For evening, go to Az-Zait in the San Lorenzon district for a unique spin on Andalusian cuisine.

Day 3:

- Visit Triananeighborhood, which is famed for its pottery and flamenco legacy. Visit the Centro Cerámica Triana to learn about the history of ceramics in the region.

- In the afternoon, go to the Monastery of San Isidoro del Campo for a more peaceful, meditative experience.

- Conclude your cultural immersion with a visit to the Alcázar Gardens, where you may unwind among the orange trees and fountains while thinking on the city's fascinating past.

Outdoor Adventure

Seville is famed for its history and culture, but it also provides several chances for outdoor enthusiasts. From bike rides to river cruises, this program is ideal for individuals who enjoy combining activity with sightseeing.

Day 1:

- Begin your day with a bicycle tour of Seville's main attractions. Most bike excursions pass via the Cathedral, Alcázar, Plaza de España, and along the Guadalquivir River.

- After lunch, head to Parque del Alamillo for an afternoon of cycling or paddle boating. This wide park is ideal for those who enjoy nature and outdoor sports.

- Finish your day with a kayak tour on the Guadalquivir River. The views from the ocean are spectacular, and it's an excellent way to unwind after a day of touring.

Day 2:

Spend the morning at Doñana National Park, a UNESCO World Heritage site located an hour from Seville. You may schedule a guided wildlife excursion to see birds, deer, and even the endangered Iberian lynx.

- Return to Seville in the afternoon and take a leisurely stroll down the Paseo de Cristóbal Colón, the riverfront promenade. Stop for a drink at Muelle de Nueva York, a riverbank pub with magnificent views.

- For dinner, visit the rooftop patio at La Azotea on Calle Jesús del Gran Poder.

Family-Friendly Trip

Seville is an excellent family destination, with numerous kid-friendly activities and attractions to discover. This itinerary is intended to keep parents and children entertained.

Day 1:

- Begin your family experience at Isla Mágica, Seville's theme park. With rides and attractions for all ages, it's a terrific way to spend a fun morning.

- After lunch, take the kids to the Acuario de Sevilla, where they can learn about marine life and get up close with sharks, turtles, and colorful fish.

- Take a stroll around Parque de María Luisa in the evening to appreciate the tranquil surroundings and let the youngsters play.

Day 2:

- Spend the morning at the Real Alcázar. The palace's lovely gardens are ideal for children to explore, and they will like the maze-like arrangement and peacocks strolling around.

- Next, go to the Casa de la Ciencia, a science museum with interactive displays that will keep kids entertained and enlightened.

- Finish the day with supper at La Brunilda, where the menu includes a variety of kid-friendly selections as well as great tapas for adults.

Budget Travel

Seville may be surprisingly inexpensive if you know where to go and what to do. This budget-friendly schedule will teach you how to get the most out of Seville while staying within your means.

Day 1:

Begin with a free walking tour of the city. Many businesses provide tip-based excursions covering significant landmarks like the Cathedral, Alcázar, and Plaza de España.

- For lunch, visit Bar Alfalfa, a quiet location famed for its affordable and tasty tapas.

- In the afternoon, pay a few euros to reach the Metropol Parasol (Las Setas) viewing platform. The views of the city are stunning.

- Finish the day with a drink at La Carbonería, a unique bar with free flamenco performances most nights.

Day 2:

- Visit the Museo del Baile Flamenco for an in-depth study at flamenco history. Admission is fairly affordable.

- Spend the afternoon walking around the Triana Market. You don't have to spend a lot of money; simply grab some fresh fruit or a snack and enjoy the lively ambiance.

- For evening, visit Bodega Santa Cruz, where the tapas are not only wonderful but also extremely affordable.

Seville in Three Days

If you have three days in Seville and want to see as much as possible, this itinerary will take you through the city's attractions while also providing opportunity for unplanned discoveries.

Day 1:

- Visit Seville Cathedral and the Giralda Tower in the morning, then the Real Alcázar in the afternoon.

- In the evening, stroll around Barrio Santa Cruz and dine at La Bartola, a charming restaurant famed for its inventive tapas.

Day 2:

- Begin with the Museo de Bellas Artes and continue to Plaza de España and Parque de María Luisa for a leisurely day.

- In the evening, attend a flamenco show at El Patio Sevillano, followed by a late-night tapas crawl in the Arenal district.

Day 3:

- Take a day excursion to Carmona or Jerez de la Frontera to discover the adjacent medieval villages.

- Return to

Seville in time for a sunset stroll along the Guadalquivir River and a farewell meal at Eslava.

Seville for the Art Lovers

Seville is a city rich in art, from Moorish palaces to cutting-edge contemporary galleries. This schedule is ideal for anyone looking to discover Seville's artistic riches.

Day 1:

- Begin at the Real Alcázar, where you'll be astounded by the Mudejar architecture and exquisite tilework.

- After lunch, pay a visit to the Museo de Bellas Artes, which houses an exceptional collection of Spanish Golden Age paintings.

- In the evening, go around the Alameda district to experience Seville's thriving street art culture.

Day 2:

- Visit Centro Andaluz de Arte Contemporáneo (CAAC) in Santa María de las Cuevas, a former monastery.

- Next, explore the Casa de Pilatos, which combines Gothic, Renaissance, and Mudejar styles.

- Wrap out the day with a visit to the Iglesia del Salvador, where you can appreciate the baroque architecture and exquisite altarpieces.

Seville is a city that has something for everyone, whether you're here for the weekend, a cultural immersion, or an art-filled trip. These itineraries are intended to help you make the most of your time in this magnificent city, but keep in mind that the best moments often occur unexpectedly. So, go a little lost and let Seville surprise you. You will not regret it!

Chapter 21

SEVILLE FOR BUDGET TRAVELERS

When I first came in Seville, I discovered that this city provides the best of all worlds: you can enjoy its rich history, gorgeous architecture, and active culture without breaking the bank. If you, like me, are always looking for methods to save a few euros without losing a wonderful experience, you've come to the perfect place. Seville is a budget traveler's paradise, thanks to its economical tapas, accessible streets, and free attractions.

The good news is that living like a king (or queen) in Seville does not require a royal budget. From breathtaking palaces to delectable dinners, there is a lot to enjoy for free or at a low cost. With some careful planning and insider knowledge, you'll be able to experience all of Seville's enchantment without breaking the bank. Let's look at how you can visit this wonderful city while staying within your budget.

Free Attractions in Seville

Many of Seville's most attractive landmarks are free to visit. The city is full of beautiful buildings, charming streets, and public places that you can explore for free. As a lover of walking without a plan, I discovered that some of the most memorable experiences in Seville was just getting lost in the city's districts.

Begin your excursion by visiting the Plaza de Españain Parque de María Luisa. This great plaza, designed for the 1929 Ibero-American Exposition, is a marvel of Moorish Revival architecture, with its massive semi-circular edifice, bright azulejos (tiles), and lovely waterway. You could easily spend hours wandering around, appreciating the bridges and people watching. If you're lucky, you might see some spontaneous flamenco performances in the plaza's corners. It's a photographer's dream, particularly if you go early in the morning before the masses gather.

After the Plaza de España, visit the Jardines de Murillo, a peaceful park ideal for a stroll or a lunchtime respite in the shade. The gardens are near to the Alcázar, so you may see the palace's tall walls while wandering among the rich flora. What is the best part? You'll feel like you're getting a glimpse into

Seville's royal past—without having to pay the Alcázar's entrance charge.

On Sundays, history buffs can enter the Seville Cathedral for free. While it can get busy, seeing the sheer scale of this Gothic beauty is well worth it. You'll also get to see Christopher Columbus' tomb, which is quite remarkable in and of itself. For the rest of the week, the cathedral's exterior is beautiful enough to view from outside. Pro tip: Take a walk around the Patio de los Naranjos, the cathedral's former mosque courtyard, for a calm escape in the city center.

And, if you're lucky enough to be in Seville during Semana Santa (Holy Week) or Feria de Abril, the streets become the primary attraction. Parades, processions, and celebrations bring the city to life, and all of them are free to attend.

Affordable Dining Options

Let's be honest: one of the best aspects of visiting Seville is the food. Fortunately, there's no need to splurge to eat well here. Tapas are the way to go if you want to try a variety of foods without spending a fortune. I spent many evenings hopping from bar to bar, eating everything from tortilla españolato jamón ibérico, all while staying within my budget.

Begin with Bodega Santa Cruz, popularly known as Las Columnas, in the heart of the Santa Cruz district. This lively, busy tapas bar is always full of locals (a good indication) and serves some of the most affordable and tasty tapas in town. The montaditos (little sandwiches) are my favorite, particularly the pringá, which is stuffed with slow-cooked pork. Remember to pair with a chilled caña (small beer). What is the best part? Most tapas here cost less than 3 euros.

Bar Alfalfa, a modest and simple restaurant near the Alameda district, is another excellent choice for budget-conscious travelers. Their salmorejo (a cold tomato-based soup) is among the best in town, and the portions are large for the price. It's also a terrific spot to sample a tosta, a toasted slice of bread with toppings ranging from goat cheese and honey to jamón and roasted peppers. After a few tapas, you'll be satisfied without breaking the bank.

If you're looking for something quick and tasty, go to Los Coloniales. It's a little more of a sit-down restaurant than the others I've listed, but the pricing are still very reasonable, and the portions are generous enough to share. Their patatas bravas and berenjenas con miel (fried eggplant with honey) are well worth the price, and the ambiance is lively but not overbearing.

Don't miss out on the Mercado de Triana, a food market right over the river in the Trianan area. You can purchase fresh local produce, cheeses, and cured meats for a picnic by the river. Furthermore, many of the shops sell prepared delicacies like as empanadas and shellfish, allowing you to grab a fast, low-cost lunch while enjoying the local environment.

Where to Stay On A Budget

Finding economical lodging in Seville should not imply sacrificing comfort or location. There are plenty of low-cost options that place you right in the thick of the activity, whether you like hostels, guesthouses, or budget hotels.

If you're traveling alone or searching for a communal setting, La Banda Rooftop Hostel is an excellent option. This hostel, near the cathedral, has a rooftop patio with stunning views of La Giralda, ideal for sunset drinks or meeting other travelers. The accommodations are clean and modern, and they provide free walking tours, which is an excellent opportunity to learn about the city without spending any money.

Hostel One Sevilla Centro offers a more relaxed atmosphere. It is located in the historic Alameda neighborhood, which is brimming with clubs, cafes, and a vibrant nightlife scene. The hostel features a nice courtyard where guests may hang out, and they provide free communal dinners, making it simple to save money on food while meeting other travelers.

If hostels are not your style, don't worry—Seville also has some reasonably priced hotels and guesthouses. Hotel Abril, located in the Santa Catalina district, provides clean and comfortable rooms at a reasonable price. It's a simple apartment, but the location is ideal for seeing the city on foot, and they even serve complimentary coffee and pastries in the morning.

Another excellent alternative is Pensión San Pancracio in the Santa Cruz neighborhood. This modest guesthouse has simple yet attractive accommodations, and the location is ideal. You're within a few steps from the Alcázar and the church, but the costs aren't outrageous.

Cheap Day Trips From Seville

One advantage of visiting Seville is its proximity to other amazing locations in Andalusia. The good news is that you don't have to spend a lot of money to have an amazing day trip. Whether you want to explore history, nature, or a combination of the two, there are numerous low-cost day trip possibilities.

Carmona is one of my favorite destinations for a quick escape from Seville. This lovely town, only a 30-minute bus ride away, is home to Roman ruins, cobblestone lanes, and breathtaking views from the Alcázar del Rey Don Pedro. What is the best part? Most of the town's attractions, including the Roman Necropolis, are free to visit, making it an excellent choice for budget travelers.

Another excellent alternative is Jerez de la Frontera, which is famous for its wine production and flamenco tradition. You can easily go to Jerez by train for less than 10 euros, and while there, you may tour one of the many bodegas (sherry wineries) or visit the Real Escuela Andaluza del Arte Ecuestre to see the famous Andalusian horses perform. If you enjoy flamenco, Jerez is the location to see an authentic performance sans the tourist crowds.

Doñana National Park is a budget-friendly option for nature lovers to explore one of Europe's most significant wetlands. While some guided excursions are expensive, there are many self-guided hiking trails that allow you to enjoy the park's natural splendor without breaking the bank. Buses to the park from Seville are cheaply affordable, making it a convenient day trip for those wishing to get away from the city's hustle.

How to Save Money on Transportation

Getting around Seville is simple—and, thankfully, affordable. The city is extremely walkable, so you can easily see most of the important sights on foot. However, if you want to cover more land or spare your legs, there are a few ways to save money on transportation.

First and foremost, Seville's public transportation system is both efficient and economical. The TUSSAM buses and trams will take you almost anyplace in the city, and a single ticket costs 1.40 euros. If you plan on taking public transportation regularly, I recommend purchasing a rechargeable travel card, which provides cheaper costs. You can buy.

You can get one at any tobacco shop or kiosk, and it's a terrific way to save a few euros if you're staying in town for a few days.

Seville also has a metro system, however not as comprehensive as the bus network. The metro is perfect if you're staying a little further afield or want to explore neighborhoods like Nervión. Tickets start at 1.35 euros, depending on how far you go.

One of my favorite ways to move around Seville on a budget is to use the Sevici bike-sharing system. For a modest cost, you may rent bikes from stations across the city and ride along Seville's network of bike lanes. It's an inexpensive and enjoyable way to explore the city, especially if you're coming during the milder months. Additionally, biking along the river or through the parks is one of the most pleasurable ways to see the attractions.

Seville is an ideal destination for budget-conscious vacationers. With free attractions, reasonable meals, and several low-cost transportation alternatives, you'll be able to explore the city without feeling as if you're missing out on anything. Seville, with its gorgeous Plaza de Españato and affordable tapas, demonstrates that a memorable trip does not require a large budget. So pack your luggage, grab your camera, and prepare to enjoy the beauty of Seville— on a budget!

Chapter 22

SEVILLE'S NIGHTLIFE

Seville doesn't only come alive when the sun shines. If anything, the city gets more mystical after nightfall. Seville's nightlife is a must-see, whether it's the golden-lit streets, the flamenco rhythms booming from tiny bars, or the murmur of lively conversations spilling out of rooftop terraces. I've spent numerous evenings roaming through Seville's vivid streets, and just when I think I've seen it all, the city surprises me again. Seville's nightlife caters to all night owls, from soul-stirring flamenco shows to late-night shopping and rooftop cocktails under the stars.

Let's learn how to make the most of your evenings in this magical city, one flamenco clap and rooftop cocktail at a time.

Flamenco Bars: Where to See Live Performances

A flamenco performance is the best way to experience the heart and spirit of Seville's culture. But be warned: flamenco is more than simply a show here; it is a way of life. The intensity of the dancers, the haunting howl of the singers, and the rapid-fire guitar strumming all contribute to a visceral, emotional experience that lingers long after the concert has ended. While flamenco can be seen in theaters, the greatest place to see its force is in one of Seville's tiny tablaos (flamenco bars).

If you're a flamenco purist, Casa de la Memoria is a must-see. This venue, housed in a wonderfully renovated 18th-century building, distills flamenco to its most essential elements. There are no gimmicks here, simply highly skilled performers who put their all into every beat, pluck, and step. The space is small, which adds to the intensity of the performance. I recall the first time I watched a show here; the room was quiet save for the rhythm of the dancers' feet and the subtle hum of the guitar. I had goosebumps from beginning to end.

El Arenal, a larger theater with more flare, provides a more polished but equally spectacular concert. This establishment has been around for decades and is one of the city's most popular flamenco locations. The performances here are larger, with dramatic lighting and exquisitely crafted costumes. It's the kind of location that makes you feel like you're entering another world. Plus, you can eat tapas and drink wine while watching the show—what could be better?

La Carbonería is ideal for anyone seeking a relaxed and off-the-beaten path experience. This bar, buried away in Santa Cruz's labyrinth, is where people congregate to hear spontaneous flamenco performances. The atmosphere is calm and bohemian, with mismatched seats, candlelit tables, and a spacious garden. Grab a glass of sangria, relax, and enjoy the show. Some nights, the performances are a little impromptu, but that's part of the fun. You never know when someone will take up a guitar and start clapping, causing the entire pub to move.

Rooftop Bars and Cocktail Lounges

Seville offers plenty of beautiful views, but there's something unique about enjoying a martini while admiring the city's famed skyline. Whether you're enjoying a romantic night out or simply want to unwind with friends, Seville's rooftop bars are the ideal place to enjoy the city's splendor.

One of my particular favorites is La Terraza del EME, which is located just across from the Seville Cathedral. Consider this: you're sipping a wonderfully constructed gin tonic while La Giralda glows in the backdrop, and the entire city appears to stretch out underneath you. This location exudes luxury and flair, with gentle lighting and stylish design that compliment the breathtaking vista. The beverages here are pricey, but the experience is well worth it. Watching the sun set behind the cathedral is an experience you won't forget.

If you want something more casual, go to Pura Vida Terraza. This rooftop bar, positioned on top of the Hotel Fontecruz, provides a relaxing ambiance with unrivaled views of the Alcázar. The atmosphere is more relaxed here, with comfortable lounge seating and a mix of residents and tourists. They frequently offer live music in the evenings, so you can sip your beverage while listening to the lovely sounds of an acoustic guitar or soulful jazz. It's an excellent place to unwind after a day spent seeing the city's attractions.

Terraza Hotel Doña María offers a bustling rooftop atmosphere. This is one of the most popular rooftop bars in the city, and with good reason. The views of the cathedral and La Giralda are stunning, particularly at night when everything is illuminated. The cocktails are innovative, and the atmosphere is constantly lively. It's the ideal place to start or conclude your night out in Seville.

Nightclubs for the Energetic Traveler

If you are the type of traveler who enjoys partying till the early hours, Seville's nightclub culture will not disappoint. The city's nightlife doesn't begin until after midnight, so come prepared for a long night. Seville's clubs feature everything from reggaeton beats to electronic dance music, catering to a diverse spectrum of musical interests and genres.

Antique Theatro is one of Seville's most famous clubs. This establishment is all about the glitz and glamour, nestled in a former theater that has been converted into a large nightclub. With its exquisite decor, velvet drapes, and chandeliers, you feel as if you've stepped onto the set of a major show. The music here is a blend of house, reggaeton, and international songs, so there is something for everyone. Just be prepared for a wait to get in—it's a popular spot, especially on weekends.

Sala Malandari is the place to be if you want to experience a more alternative vibe. This bar, located in the Alameda district, features a more diversified music roster that includes everything from indie rock to electronica. It's popular among locals looking to avoid the flashier clubs, and the ambiance is refreshingly down-to-earth. The dance floor is full until early in the morning, and the beverages are moderately priced, making it an excellent choice for a fun (and economical) night out.

Bilindois, an outdoor nightclub in Parque de María Luisa, offers the opportunity to dance beneath the stars. This open-air location is ideal for summer nights, with palm trees, glittering fairy lights, and a tropical atmosphere that seems like a tiny vacation. The music is a blend of Latin beats, house, and live

DJ performances, and the outdoor location makes it one of Seville's most popular party spots.

Night Markets and Late-night Shopping

Seville isn't known for its night markets, but if you know where to look, you can find some wonderful places to go late-night shopping and discover unique finds. One of the finest locations to start is the Alameda de Hércules neighborhood, which has a number of independent shops and boutiques that stay open late. Vintage apparel, handmade jewelry, and odd art pieces are among the items available.

During certain periods of the year, the Alameda also holds pop-up night markets, particularly during holidays and festivals. These marketplaces are ideal for perusing unique, handcrafted items such as ceramics, leather goods, and homemade soaps. Furthermore, there is always a joyful environment, with live music, food booths, and street performers adding to the excitement.

Calle Sierpe is Seville's main shopping street, and while most of the businesses close early in the evening, some stay open late on weekends. It's an excellent place to buy Andalusian goods like flamenco scarves, espadrilles, and a bottle of local sherry. There's something so fulfilling about strolling through these quaint neighborhoods after dark, especially when the lights shine overhead and the air feels chilly.

If you're a foodie like me, you must visit the Mercado Lonja del Barranco, a gourmet food market located directly on the river. While the market is well known for its food stalls, it also holds many evening events, such as craft markets and live music performances. It's the ideal place to have a bite to eat while perusing local products and handmade items.

Best Night Walks in Seville

Seville is a city designed for walking, and it's even more lovely at night. The streets are quieter, the monuments are illuminated, and the lanterns' soft glow sheds a lovely light on the city's old structures. If you aren't ready to call it a night after dinner, a midnight stroll through Seville is the ideal opportunity to see the city's attractiveness in a new light.

One of my favorite night hikes begins with the Torre del Oro, a golden tower on the banks of the Guadalquivir River. From here, take a stroll down the riverfront on the Paseo de Cristóbal Colón, where the city lights reflect in the water. The view of Triana across the river is especially lovely at night, with its vibrant buildings and active ambiance. If you continue walking, you will ultimately reach the Puente de Isabel II, also known as the Triana Bridge. This renowned bridge is illuminated at night and provides a breathtaking view of the river and city.

For a more atmospheric walk, visit the Barrio Santa Cruz, Seville's old Jewish enclave. The tight, twisting alleyways are fascinating during the day, but at night, they take on an entirely new sense of mystique. There's something romantic about meandering through these ancient lanes, where the only noises are distant murmurs of conversations and the occasional echo of your footsteps. You'll pass by secret courtyards, beautiful iron gates, and even catch a peek of a private garden via an open window. It's like going through a dream in which time appears to stop still.

If you're feeling daring, you may join one of Seville's ghost tours, which take you around the Barrio Santa Cruz and other sections of the city. These tours delve into Seville's ghostly folklore and haunted history, and regardless of whether you believe in ghosts, the stories are interesting (and a little creepy).

Seville's nightlife provides something for everyone, whether you want to see an intimate flamenco performance, have a rooftop beverage with a view, or dance the night away beneath the stars. After dark, the city comes alive in a whole new way, and you don't want to miss out on this side of Seville. So gather your friends, your dancing shoes, and your spirit of adventure, and prepare to enjoy Seville's dynamic, passionate, and spectacular nightlife.

Chapter 23

PACKING FOR A TRIP TO SEVILLE

Packing for Seville can seem like an art form. Do you prioritize comfort for all the walking you'll be doing, or should you harness your inner Andalusian and go for style? And then there's the weather—if you've ever visited Seville in the summer, you know that going outside is like walking into an oven. Having spent a lot of time in this sun-drenched city, I've made all of the packing mistakes—too many jackets in the spring, shoes that weren't designed for cobblestones, and don't even get me started on the time I forgot sunscreen. So, let's make sure you're ready for your vacation to Seville, from smart streetwear to must-have travel devices you'll thank me after.

Let's break it down and figure out what you'll need to bring to make your vacation to Seville as comfortable and pleasurable as possible.

Seasonal Packing Guide

Seville's climate is all about extremes. Summers can be hot, with temperatures exceeding 40°C (104°F), but winters are pleasant, with shockingly cold mornings and evenings. What you pack depends heavily on the time of year, so here's a handy checklist to help you figure it out.

Spring (March-May) is one of the greatest periods to visit Seville. The weather is pleasant but not hot, and the city comes alive with events such as Semana Santa and Feria de Abril. Pack light layers like trousers, flowy dresses, and breathable shirts or blouses. Mornings and nights might be cool, so pack a light jacket or sweater. If you're going during Feria, bring your best outfit; Seville takes fashion seriously during the fair!

Summer (June to September): Let's be honest: Seville in the summer is no joke. The heat is extreme, especially in July and August, so pack appropriately. Consider breathable textiles such as linen and cotton to avoid suffocating in the 40-degree heat. Dresses, shorts, and lightweight shirts are your best friends. Sunglasses, a wide-brimmed hat, and high-quality sunscreen are not optional. yet, make sure your sandals are comfy enough to stroll in while yet looking chic enough to fit in with the Sevillanos. You may also want to bring a little hand fan (I once bought one at a market and it saved my life), because you will be fanning yourself beneath the blazing heat.

Autumn (October to November) is a beautiful time to visit Seville, with pleasant days and colder evenings. Pack similarly to spring: lightweight layers, but remember to bring a jacket for those cool evenings. Seville's fall fashion is fashionable but comfy, so a gorgeous scarf or shawl can add a touch of local character to your outfit.

Winter (December to February): While Seville's winters are milder than those in northern Europe or the United States, they may still be rather cold, particularly in the mornings and evenings. Pack a warm coat, especially if you get cold quickly. You'll also want some warm sweaters and long pants. During the day, temperatures can reach the upper teens (Celsius), thus layering is essential. Don't be deceived by the beautiful skies; those shadowed, tiny alleyways might be rather cold!

Essentials for Sightseeing

Seville is a walking city, so bring along some comfy basics for your tour excursions. You'll be walking a lot while visiting Santa Cruz's winding alleys, ascending La Giralda, and getting lost in the Alcázar gardens. Here is what you should bring:

- Comfortable shoes: This is obvious, but it cannot be stressed. The streets of Seville are primarily cobblestone, so you'll be walking a lot. Bring a pair of well-cushioned sneakers or walking shoes that can handle uneven terrain. If you like to combine comfort and style, choose a pair of trendy flats or fashionable sandals that nevertheless provide some support. I once wore flimsy sandals to Plaza de España, and by the end of the day, my feet were ready to strike.

- Daypack or crossbody bag: You'll need something lightweight and practical to transport your essentials— wallet, sunscreen, water bottle, and, of course, camera or phone. A compact crossbody purse is great for securing your stuff while navigating crowded streets and markets.

- Water bottle: Seville can get hot, especially during the summer, so staying hydrated while sightseeing is crucial. Most restaurants will happily refill your water bottle, and there are a few public fountains throughout the city, but they might be difficult to locate.

- Sunscreen and sunglasses: Even in the milder months, Seville's sun can be harsh, so protect yourself with a high-SPF sunscreen and a decent pair of sunglasses. I've spent enough time in Seville blinking at the sun to realize that missing your sunglasses is a novice mistake.

- Portable fan (in summer): As I previously stated, if you're visiting during the summer, a little, handheld fan is a game changer. Locals will also use them, and it's a simple, stylish method to remain cool on those hot afternoon walks.

Comfort vs Style: What Locals Wear

Seville is a city where people dress to impress, even on a casual evening paseo. The Sevillanos have a knack for looking effortlessly fashionable while remaining comfortable, so if you want to blend in (and avoid appearing too touristy), achieve a balance between comfort and flair.

Even in the summer, women frequently wear flowy dresses, attractive shoes, and lightweight scarves. If you travel during the shoulder seasons, you'll see plenty of fashionable ankle boots, blazers, and trench coats—ideal for cooler evenings. I've found that people in Seville avoid extremely casual outfits during the day, so keep your gym clothes and flip-flops at home unless you're going to the beach.

For males, chinos or well-fitted trousers with a linen shirt or polo will help you blend in with the locals quickly. Even in the heat, the men of Seville manage to look professional while remaining comfortable. Lightweight sneakers or leather sandals are suitable for walking, as long as they are comfortable.

What if you're going out at night? Sevillanos go above and above, even when it comes to tapas. A lovely dress or elegant jumpsuit for women, or a button-up shirt and dark trousers for men, will put you right at ease amid the city's trendy pubs and restaurants.

Packing for Day Trips

Seville is conveniently located for day visits to adjacent attractions such as Córdoba, Jerez de la Frontera, and Doñana National Park. While you won't need to pack a separate bag for these quick journeys, there are a few items you should have in your daypack to ensure you're ready.

- Comfortable walking shoes: Again, this is essential—most day trips from Seville include a lot of walking, whether you're visiting the Mezquita in Córdoba or the Roman ruins in Carmona.

- Light jacket or scarf: Although it is warm in Seville, some areas, particularly those near the shore, can be breezy. A light jacket or scarf will keep you comfortable, especially in the spring and fall.

- Travel handbook or map: If you're like me and enjoy learning about the areas you visit, pack a compact guidebook or download an offline map of the area. It's always useful to have a reference, especially while exploring smaller places where Wi-Fi may be unreliable.

- Snacks and water:While there is no shortage of delicious cuisine wherever you travel, it's always a good idea to bring a little snack or two, especially if you're hiking or visiting a distant location. A bag of almonds or a piece of fruit might provide a rapid energy boost.

Must-Have Travel Accessories for Seville

In this digital age, bringing smart gadgets might make your journey easier and more pleasurable. Here are a few must-have gadgets that I've found really useful while navigating Seville's winding streets and ancient landmarks:

- Portable charger: Between shooting photos, using Google Maps, and looking up restaurant reviews, your phone's battery might soon drain. A portable charger is vital, especially if you'll be exploring for the entire day and won't have time to recharge.

- A camera or smartphone with a good camera: Seville is extremely attractive, and you'll want to record its beauty at every turn. Whether you're using your phone or a DSLR camera, be sure you have enough storage space and a spare battery. I've taken numerous photos of Plaza de Españaalone, filling up my phone's storage space.

- Bluetooth headphones: Whether you're listening to an audio guide, listening to your favorite podcast while walking down the river, or simply filtering out the noise on a train ride to Córdoba, Bluetooth headphones are an excellent travel accessory.

- Travel adapter:If you are coming from outside of Europe, you will require a European plug.

Adapter for charging your devices. Believe me, you do not want to be stuck with a dead phone and no way to charge it.

Packing for Seville involves striking a balance between comfort and Andalusian style. With the correct gear and some forethought, you'll be ready for anything Seville throws at you—whether it's a last-minute day excursion to Cádiz, a spontaneous flamenco show, or simply roaming the Alcázargardens in the afternoon sun. So pack smartly, light, and prepare to experience the lively energy of this unique city. Enjoy your travels!

Chapter 24

CONCLUSION: THE MAGIC OF SEVILLE

As I sit here reflecting on my time in Seville, I am reminded of what makes this city so unique. There's something nearly mystical about Seville. It's a location where history and current life mingle seamlessly, where every street corner seems to whisper centuries-old secrets, and where life moves at its own distinct pace. It's a city that forces you to slow down, take a deep breath, and genuinely appreciate the present. Whether you're sipping a glass of sherry in a lively tapas bar, meandering through the lush gardens of the Alcázar, or watching the sunset from a rooftop terrace, Seville has a way of drawing you in and making you feel like you've discovered a tiny slice of heaven.

Reflecting on Seville's Unique Charm

Seville is a city that makes an impression on your soul. It's the type of place that stays with you long after you've left, bringing back memories of balmy afternoons spent walking its narrow alleys or the vivid colors of flamenco dancers whirling in the dark light of a tablao. Seville's charm is obvious. It's in the people, who greet you with a grin and a warm heart. The aroma of orange blossoms wafts through the air in the spring. It's the food—oh, the food! that elevates every meal into an occasion.

Seville has always appealed to me because it feels lively while remaining strongly anchored in its traditions. You can walk through a modern area of the city and be taken back in time in minutes, standing before a Moorish palace or a magnificent Gothic church. It's a city where the past is not only preserved, but also lived. Every flamenco performance, festival, and local conversation carries the weight of centuries of tradition. That's what makes Seville so magical: it's a location where time moves differently, where the ancient and new coexist in perfect harmony.

Make the Most of Your Time in the City

If there's one thing I've learnt from my time in Seville, it's to not rush. Seville is not a city that values speed. Sure, you could see the key sights in a few days, but that's not how Seville is supposed to be experienced. Take your time. Sit in a café and people-watch for a bit. Wander the streets without a specific destination in mind. You'll be astounded by the minor discoveries you uncover along the way—a secret patio, a tiny bar offering the greatest jamón you've ever had, or a street musician singing a haunting melody that stops you in your tracks.

One of my favorite activities to do in Seville is pasear, a leisurely nighttime promenade that is an important element of Andalusian culture. The inhabitants practice this regularly, especially in the early evening, when the heat of the day has subsided and the streets are bathed in a gentle, golden glow. I've lost count of how many times I've wound myself in a new part of town simply by following my feet, frequently discovering a lovely cathedral, a tucked-away garden, or an atmospheric tavern where I've spent hours conversing with locals over a glass of Tinto de Verano.

Must-See Spots Before You Leave

While there are plenty of fantastic locations to see in Seville, there are a handful that you simply must not miss. These are the sites that encapsulate the soul of the city, and they will make you fall in love with Seville all over again.

1. The Real Alcázar: If you haven't previously seen this breathtaking palace, make it your top priority before leaving. The combination of Mudejar, Gothic, Renaissance, and Baroque architecture is beautiful, and the gardens provide a calm sanctuary away from the city's hustle and bustle. You'll feel like royalty as you meander around the enormous halls and courtyards—don't forget to take a moment to sit by the reflection ponds and soak in the beauty of the site.

2. Plaza de España is a well-known tourist attraction in Seville. The majesty of this semi-circular plaza, complete with vivid tiles and imposing bridges, must be seen in person to be properly appreciated. Rent a rowboat and float along the canal, or simply walk around and observe the beautiful tilework representing each of Spain's provinces.

3. Seville Cathedral and La Giralda: You haven't truly experienced Seville until you've climbed the ramps of La Giralda and enjoyed the city's panoramic views from the summit. The cathedral itself is breathtaking, with its expansive interior, magnificent stained glass windows, and Christopher Columbus' tomb. Spend some time roaming around the Patio de los Naranjos, a pleasant courtyard full of orange trees.

4. Triana: To enjoy Seville's true charm, cross the Puente de Isabel II into the vibrant neighborhood of Triana. Triana, known for its pottery, flamenco tradition, and colorful street life, has the feel of a hamlet within the metropolis. Explore the Triana Market, eat lunch on Calle Betis, and take in the local culture in this vibrant neighborhood.

5. Metropol Parasol: Known as "Las Setas," this modern architectural masterpiece provides a unique perspective of Seville. Climb to the summit for panoramic views of the city, and take in the contrast between Seville's old-world elegance and this contemporary timber tower. It's an excellent spot to see the sunset, with the city spreading underneath you in all its splendor.

Final Travel Tips for the Perfect Trip

As you prepare to say farewell to Seville, here are a few last travel suggestions to make your trip even more enjoyable.

- Take your time with meals: In Seville, eating is a communal activity. Meals are meant to be enjoyed, and hurrying through tapas simply does not feel right. Take your time, order a variety of foods, and enjoy the lively conversation that is sure to occur around you. If you haven't already, try salmorejo, espinacas con garbanzos, and torrijas, a traditional local dessert.

- Get lost on purpose: Some of Seville's most magical moments occur when you don't follow a map. Allow yourself to explore, especially in places like Santa Cruz and Macarena. You'll come across calm plazas, secluded gardens, and possibly even a secret courtyard that feels like your own personal discovery.

- Dress for the occasion: Sevillanos are elegant even when they're merely taking a stroll. If you want to fit in, bring something a little nicer for evening outings.

Even a modest scarf or a great pair of shoes can improve your appearance, especially if you're going to one of Seville's many rooftop bars or flamenco performances.

- Enjoy the siesta: Seville can get hot, especially during the summer months. Don't resist it; accept the native tradition of having a siesta during the warmest portion of the day. Use this time to unwind, rejuvenate, and prepare for the evening ahead. After all, the city comes alive at night.

- Download important apps: If you want to spend an evening at home, make sure you have Google Maps, Sevici (the city's bike-sharing service), and Glovoor Uber Eats. These will make getting around the city and eating on the move much easier.

A Warm Farewell from Seville

As you pack your luggage and prepare to leave this magnificent city, take one last look around. Seville has a way of catching your heart, and I'm sure you'll want to return one day. Perhaps it's the warm glow of the Giralda sunset, the distant sound of flamenco clapping, or the simple pleasure of sitting in a plaza with a glass of wine in hand. Whatever it is, Seville makes a lasting impression.

So, as you leave for the airport or train station, remember that Seville is saying goodbye to you while simultaneously quietly whispering, "Come back soon."

Because once you've felt the charm of this city, it's impossible to stay away for long.

Hasta luego and safe travels. Hope your recollections of Seville are as warm and bright as the city itself.

Chapter 25

USEFUL RESOURCES

Traveling to Seville is an adventure full of vibrant culture, delectable cuisine, and breathtaking architecture. However, like with any journey, having the correct resources available can make all the difference. After spending a lot of time navigating Seville's maze of streets, dealing with the occasional travel hitch, and immersing myself in the city's culture, I've compiled this handy addendum to help you make the most of your trip. Whether you need emergency contact information, a few Spanish phrases, or a map that will not lead you into a maze of medieval lanes (unless that's what you're looking for), these resources have you covered.

Emergency Contacts

Let's start with the essentials. Hopefully, you won't need these, but having emergency contact information is always a good idea. Knowing who to call and where to go when things don't go as planned can significantly reduce stress in a challenging scenario.

- Emergency Number (Spain's 112 Service): This is the number to call for any type of emergency, whether it's police, fire, or medical. Operators speak English, and the service is available around the clock.

- Police: 091 (National Police); 092 (Local Police)

- Ambulance: 061.

- Pharmacies: In Spain, pharmacies have a rotating schedule for after-hours services. Look for the "Farmacia de Guardia" sign on the door of a local pharmacy to identify one that is open around the clock. You may also verify which pharmacies are open at www.farmaciasdeguardia.com.

- Seville Tourist Information: Tourist Police are helpful if you lose your passport or require assistance as a tourist. You may locate them in Plaza de San Francisco or phone +34 954 221 171.

- Hospitals in Seville: Hospital Universitario Virgen del Rocío, located at Av. Manuel Siurot, 41013 Seville. It is one of the biggest hospitals in Andalusia. Another alternative is Hospital Quirónsalud Sagrado Corazón, a private hospital on Av. de la Palmera, 41012 Seville.

- Embassies and Consulates: If you are from outside the EU and require consular help, make sure you have the contact information for your country's nearest embassy or consulate. This information is typically available on your country's government travel website or by conducting an online search.

Maps and Navigation Tools

Getting lost in Seville may be a joyful adventure or a never-ending maze of little alleyways. Fortunately, there are numerous apps and websites available to assist you in navigating the city without becoming frustrated.

- Google Maps: This is my go-to tool for navigating Seville. It is accurate and contains public transportation, walking routes, and points of interest. Pro tip: Before you explore through Triana or Santa Cruz, get an offline map because Wi-Fi can be intermittent.

www.google.com/maps

- Moovit: If you intend to use Seville's public transit, this app is ideal for real-time bus and tram schedules. It will assist you figure out when your next ride will arrive and how to navigate the city efficiently.

www.moovitapp.com

- TUSSAM App: Seville's public bus system has its own app that allows you to check schedules, routes, and even top up your Tarjeta Multiviaje (multi-trip card). It's quite beneficial if you plan on taking the bus frequently during your trip.

www.tussam.es

- Sevici: If riding about Seville appeals to you, download this app. Sevici is the city's bike-sharing program, and the app displays available bikes, docking stations, and your journey history.

www.sevici.es

- Citymapper: Another great navigation software, Citymapper helps you locate the best route from point A to point B, whether it's by foot, bus, bike, or tram. It's simple to use and makes navigating the city effortless.

www.citymapper.com

Additional Reading and References

For those who enjoy delving deeply into a place's history, culture, and stories, here are some recommended books and websites to supplement your Seville experience. These are excellent reads for the airline ride or a relaxing afternoon in a plaza with a coffee (or glass of sherry) in hand.

- Elizabeth Nash's book "Seville: A Cultural and Literary History" This book delves deep into Seville's history, from its Roman origins to its current liveliness. It's ideal if you want to go beyond the usual tourist attractions and learn the cultural importance of what you're seeing.

- Giles Tremlett's book "Ghosts of Spain: Travels Through Spain and Its Silent Past" While not entirely centered on Seville, this book delves into Spain's recent history and cultural identity. It's a fascinating read that sheds insight on some of the country's more convoluted history.

- John Hooper's "The New Spaniards" This is a detailed overview of Spain's modern political and cultural scene. It's an excellent book for anyone interested in learning more about the country than the preconceptions of flamenco, siestas, and fiestas suggest.

- Sevilla City Tourism: The official Seville tourism website contains a wealth of useful information, event listings, and data on tours and attractions. It's an excellent resource for current information, both before and during your journey.

 www.visitasevilla.es

- Andalucia.com: This website covers the entire area of Andalusia but also contains a wealth of information on Seville. It's ideal for organizing day trips, discovering hidden gems, and getting local recommendations.

 www.andalucia.com

Useful Local Phrases

While many people in Seville speak English, particularly in tourist areas, knowing a few basic Spanish words can be extremely useful. It will not only help you manage everyday circumstances, but it will also allow you to engage with locals and demonstrate your willingness to learn their language. Here are some key phrases that you may find useful:

- Hola– Hello

- Buenos días– Good morning

- Buenas tardes– Good afternoon

- Gracias– Thank you

- Por favor– Please

- Lo siento– I'm sorry

- ¿Cuánto cuesta?– How much does it cost?

- La cuenta, por favor– The bill, please

- Una caña, por favor– A small beer, please (this one will come in handy)

- ¿Dónde está…?– Where is…?

- Baños– Bathrooms

- Agua sin gas– Still water (important if you don't want sparkling!)

- No hablo español muy bien– I don't speak Spanish very well (A little honesty never hurts!)

Glossary

Here's a glossary of terminology you're likely to encounter during your journey. Many of these are peculiar to Seville or Andalusia and will make navigating the local culture easier.

- Tapas are small dishes of food that are frequently shared among friends. Popular tapas in Seville include jamón ibérico (Iberian ham), tortilla española (Spanish omelette), and garlic shrimp.

- Paseo: A leisurely evening stroll that Sevillanos enjoy, particularly during the summer months. It's an excellent way to experience the city at its most active.

- Flamenco is a passionate art form that blends singing, guitar, and dance. Flamenco is strongly ingrained in Andalusian culture and a must-see in Seville.

- Azulejos: Decorative ceramic tiles found everywhere in Seville, including building walls, street signs, and fountains. They are a symbol of Seville's Moorish and Renaissance architectural traditions.

- Semana Santa: Holy Week in Seville is one of Spain's most important religious occasions, with solemn processions and celebrations held across the city. It occurs during the week leading up to Easter.

- Feria de Abril is Seville's annual spring fair, held two weeks following Easter. Flamenco dance, horse parades, and plenty of rebujito (a sherry and soda drink) are among the highlights of the week-long event.

- Tinto de Verano: A famous summer beverage in Seville made from red wine and lemon soda. It's comparable to sangria but lighter and more refreshing, ideal for hot afternoons.

I hope this appendix of valuable materials allows you to make the most of your time in Seville. Whether you're brushing up on your Spanish, getting lost with an excellent map, or doing some extra reading, these resources will make you feel prepared and thrilled for your vacation. Enjoy every moment in this intriguing city—Seville is eager to greet you!

When visiting Seville, one of Spain's most beautiful towns, you'll want to know where to stay, eat, drink, and see the top sights. Here's a complete guide with all the information you need to ensure you don't miss anything during your visit From chic hotels and top dining spots to the most popular pubs and historic landmarks, this guide will help you navigate Seville like a local.

Addresses and Locations for Popular Accommodation

Seville has a diverse choice of accommodations, from luxury hotels to lovely boutique guesthouses. Here are some of our favorite recommendations, along with addresses and website links for simple booking.

1. Hotel Alfonso XIII: Address: Calle San Fernando, 2, 41004 Sevilla. This historic hotel, regarded as one of Spain's most magnificent, provides lavish suites with stunning views of the city's most prominent sites.

2. EME Catedral Mercer Hotel - Location: Calle Alemanes, 27, 41004 Sevilla This elegant boutique hotel, located in the heart of Seville, right next to the Cathedral, offers modern rooms and a rooftop pool with breathtaking views of La Giralda.

3. Hotel Casa 1800 Sevilla - Address: Calle Rodrigo Caro, 6, 41004 Sevilla - A boutique hotel with a classic Andalusian flavor, located in the Santa Cruz neighborhood, close to the Cathedral and Alcázar. - Website: www.hotelcasa1800sevilla.com.

4. Hotel Inglaterra - Address: Plaza Nueva, 7, 41001 Sevilla - One of Seville's most prominent hotels, delivering classic elegance in the city center with convenient access to shopping and dining. - Website: www.hotelinglaterra.es.

5. La Banda Rooftop Hostel - Address: Calle Dos de Mayo, 16, 41001 Sevilla A low-cost choice suitable for young tourists. It has inexpensive dorm rooms and a rooftop terrace with views of Seville Cathedral.

- Website address: www.labandahostel.com

Addresses and Locations of Popular Restaurants and Cafés

Seville takes food very seriously. There are fantastic dining options around every corner, ranging from classic tapas to sophisticated Spanish food. Here are some renowned destinations you should not miss.

1. El Rinconcillo - Calle Gerona, 40, 41003 Sevilla - Established in 1670, this is Seville's oldest tapas tavern, where you can eat classic Andalusian delicacies like espinacas con garbanzos (spinach with chickpeas) and salmorejo. - Website: www.elrinconcillo.es.

2. La Brunilda Tapas - Calle Galera 5, 41001 Sevilla. A hidden gem serving inventive tapas with a modern twist. It's always busy, so arrive early or expect to wait for a table.

 - Website address: www.labrunildatapas.com

3. Eslava - Address: Calle Eslava, 3, 41002 Sevilla A highly recommended tapas bar in the Alameda neighborhood, noted for inventive delicacies such as slow-cooked pig ribs and honeyed foie gras.

4. Ovejas Negras - Calle Hernando Colón, 8, 41004 Sevilla - A trendy tapas bar in Seville that serves modern Spanish cuisine in a dynamic and hip

environment. - Website:
www.ovejasnegrastapas.com.

5. Confitería La Campana: Address: Calle Sierpes, 1,
41004 Sevilla. A historic café and pastry business,
ideal for a mid-morning coffee and tarta de San
Marcos. A must-visit for fans of classic Spanish
pastries.

  - Website: www.confiterialacampana.com.

Addresses and Locations of Popular Bars and Clubs

When night falls, Seville's lively nightlife comes alive.
Whether you're looking for rooftop bars with
breathtaking views or clubs to dance the night away,
these are some of the best options.

1. La Terraza del EME - Calle Alemanes, 27, 41004
Sevilla - A rooftop bar with stunning views of the
Giralda. It's the ideal place to drink a martini while
watching the sunset over the city.

2. La Carbonería - Address: Calle Céspedes, 21A,
41004 Sevilla This bohemian pub in the heart of
Santa Cruz is well-known for its nightly flamenco
concerts. Grab a drink and take in the real Andalusian
atmosphere.

  - Website address: www.lacarboneria.net.

3. Antique Theatro - Address: Calle Matemáticos Rey
Pastor y Castro, s/n, 41092 Sevilla - Seville's most

popular nightclub, housed in an antique theater. It features opulent décor and a lively dance floor with a mix of international and Spanish favorites.

- Website address: www.antiquetheatro.com

4. Bilindo: Address: Parque de María Luisa, 41013 Sevilla. An open-air nightclub in the picturesque Maria Luisa Park, perfect for summer nights. It has a more casual mood, with a blend of Latin and house music.

5. Bar Americano @ Hotel Alfonso XIII - Address: Calle San Fernando, 2, 41004 Sevilla For a classy evening drink, visit the Bar Americano at the elegant Hotel Alfonso XIII. It evokes the glamour of the 1920s while still providing a polished cocktail experience.

Addresses and Locations of the Top Attractions

No visit to Seville is complete without seeing its famed sights. Here are the top destinations that should be on every traveler's itinerary, along with their locations and websites for further information.

1. Seville Cathedral and La Giralda - Location: Av. de la Constitución, s/n, 41004 Sevilla. The largest Gothic cathedral in the world, and the La Giralda tower provides panoramic views of the city. Don't miss the opportunity to ascend to the top!

- Site: www.catedraldesevilla.es.

2. Real Alcázar of Seville - Address: Patio de Banderas, s/n, 41004 Sevilla. This gorgeous royal house, a UNESCO World Heritage Site, is one of Seville's most popular attractions, boasting Mudejar architecture and lush gardens.

- Website address: www.alcazarsevilla.org

3. Plaza de España - Location: Av. Isabel la Católica, 41004 Sevilla This enormous plaza is a Renaissance Revival architectural marvel and one of Seville's most recognizable sights. It's also an excellent location for a lovely boat cruise.

- Website: www.visitasevilla.es/lugar-interes/plaza-de-espana.

4. Metropol Parasol (Las Setas) - Location: Pl. de la Encarnación, s/n, 41003 Sevilla A modern architectural masterpiece that provides panoramic views of Seville. Its timber structure and rooftop pathways are ideal for sunset viewing.

5. Torre del Oro - Address: Paseo de Cristóbal Colón, s/n, 41001 Sevilla. This 13th-century watchtower on the Guadalquivir River is a reminder of Seville's maritime heritage. You can ascend to the top for spectacular views of the River.

This guide of Seville's best hotels, restaurants, pubs, and sights will help you make the most of your visit. Whether you're here for a weekend or a longer stay, knowing where to go is essential for experiencing everything this lovely city has to offer.

Printed in Great Britain
by Amazon